One Ship Sails East

by
Cameron Townsend and Others

Summer Institute of Linguistics
Waxhaw, North Carolina

*"One ship sails East
and another West
In the self-same wind that blows.
It's the set of the sail
and not the gale
That determines the way it goes."*

–Ella Wheeler Wilcox

Acknowledgements

The pieces by Cameron Townsend in this book are transcriptions of recorded talks he gave to members of the Summer Institute of Linguistics. They have been edited by Richard Pittman.

The original tapes and transcripts are in the Townsend Archives at the JAARS Center, Waxhaw, NC. They were collected by Cal Hibbard and transcribed by Violet Dunbar. Marge Bondurant typed the edited set, and Nancy Duncan organized and composed the collection, with help from John King.

Gladys Zellmer supervised the second reproduction and then entered the entire volume onto computer for this edition. Beverly Brodhacker saw the first run through the press, and Brian Tenny this latest one. RSP is responsible for general editing and for the specific pieces identified by those initials. Vivian Robbins spent many hours checking the penultimate version. Final proofing was done by Joyce Gullman and Thelma Johnston.

Richard S. Pittman
September, 1987

Table of Contents

Preface

Creaking and groaning complaints growled from the gears of the crowded bus in which I was riding up India's Eastern Ghats. The narrow, twisting, steep-grade highway taxed the driver's skill to keep us safely on course.

No wonder we stopped, halfway up, to pay homage to the local deity, hoping for his protection the rest of the way. And no wonder every passenger contributed a few coins to the offering plate which was passed by an old priest who boarded the bus with his little granddaughter.

I had scruples against it. Neither wanting nor seeking the benediction of the spirit of the mountain, I was not about to put money in the plate. But it was equally obvious that everyone expected me to. If I failed, I would be the Jonah who might cause the bus to dive over the brink into the abyss, with harm not only to me but also to all. What to do?

I knew that a constructive alternative was called for. But what? Praying earnestly to *my* God I groped for help. It came! In a lunch which some kind soul had packed for me were two lovely cookies. I remembered them just as the collection dish reached me. With a great smile I put them on it and said to the little girl, "These are for *you*." Her radiant answering smile assured me that she understood and that she expected to eat them after the bus had left.

How much we all need such illustrative helps. Excursions abroad, whether for work or for rest, can be disaster without them. Providentially Cameron Townsend and others have given us a rich store of them. International and cross-cultural relations can benefit much from knowing these materials.

This is the second volume of material by Cameron Townsend and colleagues illustrating the principles and practice of international relations as he urged that they be applied by the Summer Institute of Linguistics. That there has often been a gap between competence and performance we would all admit. We would also allege, however, that there is a timeless and universal quality to the principles which recommend them for application far beyond the time and place of SIL.

It is in that confidence that they are here presented.

Richard S. Pittman
September, 1987

I

Chart and Compass

A fixed chart and a floating compass needle
may seem incongruous to a philosopher,
but not to a mariner.

-RSP

Coffee for
the Truck Driver

He Emphasized Our Honesty.

"Bless those who persecute you; bless and curse not. Rejoice with those who rejoice, and weep with those who weep. Be of the same mind one toward another." (That is your teammate.) "Mind not high things, but go along with men of low esteem. Be not wise in your own conceits. Recompense to no man evil for evil. Provide things honest in the sight of all men." Rom. 12:14-17.

We had not been working very many years in Mexico when a newspaper editor wrote an article about us. He did not have much to say about our linguistic research, nor much to say about our literacy, nor much to say about our love for the Indians. What he emphasized was our honesty. He was amazed to see that we practiced the precept: "Provide things honest in the sight of all men."

During the years which elapsed after he wrote that article, our reputation for honesty has continued. Some couple years ago, for example, I was requested by a radio man to take a radio to Mexico. I was going from Charlotte to Mexico City, and the instructions were, "Be sure to pay import duty on this, because it is going to stay in Mexico."

So when I got out at the airport in Mexico City and they were going through my luggage, I said, "This radio is going to stay here. I am going through to Colombia but the radio stays, so I want to pay duty on it."

The man said, "Aren't you with the Summer Institute of Linguistics?"

I said, "Yes."

He said, "Well, you do not have to pay duty."

"But I was told by our radio man to pay duty this time."

He said, "Well, I'll go see the chief."

So he told the chief the problem. The chief said, "Oh, that's the way those folks are. Do not accept it."

"Provide things honest in the sight of all men." "If it be possible, as far as you are concerned, live peaceably with all men. Dearly beloved, avenge not yourselves, but instead let God's anger do it. For it is written, vengeance is mine, I will repay, saith the Lord. Therefore if thine enemy hunger, feed him, if he thirst, give him drink, for in so doing thou shalt heap coals of fire on his head. Be not overcome by evil, but overcome evil with good."

My boy Bill some years ago said: "Daddy, who wants to heap coals of fire on anybody's head?"

So I like to say now, "Pour water on his gun powder. Make it so that he cannot do you harm or possibly will not even want to."

We're in the People Business.

People constitute the big problem that confronts us on any field. If an official calls on us, for example, or comes to the Center, somebody must take time to attend to that official and stick right with him. When guests come, we must not be too busy to take care of them. Push aside your work. Of course, there are people who will abuse that. You will catch on to that and you will find ways of excusing yourself. But ordinarily, when a visitor comes, push aside your work, and take care of him.

How are we dealing with our employees? I feel very

strongly that we should pay the top wage of the area. Sometimes we have problems in this regard, because the patrones, who have been accustomed to having the Indians work for them, do not want the Indian to get a good wage. If you pay a good wage to that Indian, that bothers the patron. But the principle to follow is to pay a sufficient wage so that you will be considered upright. In many cultural minorities, one of the major sins is stinginess. That is a sin. Another sin is anger. So do not get angry and do not be stingy with your employees.

In Colombia, and I think the same holds true for Brazil and other places, always be ready to offer a cup of coffee to a truck driver who comes to deliver goods or packages from the capital. Always invite him to take a cup of coffee. I found that some truck drivers were coming to our Center in Colombia and were not being invited to coffee. Why? Everyone was busy on his assignment. So I had to ask that whenever a truck driver came, if there was no one prepared to serve him coffee, would they please let Elaine know so she could serve him. Have him come down the hill. A little attention like that will smooth out a lot of trouble.

One of our men was rather stern with a truck driver because he had brought a lot of passengers on top of our freight. The freight included goods which could get damaged because of people walking on top of them. If you happen to order butter, which may be available and may not, it is a prize article, and you do not want someone to walk on it. Anyhow, our man was stern with the driver, who proceeded to blow up. "You foreigners come down here and try to order us around," he stormed.

Fortunately our radio man, when he saw what was happening, came running over and said, "Say, it's about meal time. Won't you come and have dinner with us?"

Well, the truck driver was amazed at an invitation to come have dinner. But that calmed things down.

Treat your employees with consideration. Never be suspicious of them. If you are suspicious, do not let them know it; to show you are suspicious is an insult to them. If you find definitely that they are stealing from you, find a way to let them go without making a scene, if you possibly can. Try to let them save face.

Do not do your own cooking, your own washing of clothes, when you can employ someone inexpensively. Do your linguistic work. That means you are going to have a maid around the house at least half of the day.

It is very easy to suspect, "Oh, that maid took it." You have probably lost it yourself some place. You have probably mislaid it. But you ask, "Did you take that?" and it is awfully hard to win her back.

Love Never Fails.

How do we handle those who are antagonistic, those who oppose us? What are we to do? Well, God gives us a prescription. If that foe is hungry, feed him. If he is thirsty, give him drink. If he insults you, pray for him. Overcome evil with good. It does not pay to treat a person as an enemy. Do not let him think that you consider him an enemy.

One time in an Indian village in Guatemala some men broke into a place where the believers were holding a service and forced them to leave. They took the organ and threw it out in the coffee farm. They said, "Do not ever come back again to hold Gospel services in this town."

I was up in the mountains when I heard about it, so I went down to see what could be done. I said to one of the national workers, "Let's go over and hold a service."

He said, "But they said they would mob us if we ever came to hold a service again."

I said, "Well, let's go and have a service."

He said, "All right." So we went.

We went to where the mob had broken in and forced the believers to leave. I went to the owners of the home and said, "Is it all right if we hold a service?"

"Well, it will be at your own risk."

"All right," I said. "We will have a service here." About an hour and a half or two hours before the service was to start, I said to the national worker, "Let's go out and invite folks." We started down the street. At every corner, men had gathered with machetes. I greeted them like long-lost brothers.

I thought I was getting along pretty well until I looked at my companion, the national worker. He was angry and fearful. I thought, my goodness, he is inviting trouble. So as soon as we got back to the place which was going to serve as the chapel, I said, "You stay here and receive the folks as they come. I will go alone from now on." So I went in the opposite direction.

I would greet these men, with their long knives, cordially. I got down to the central square. There the kids were playing basketball. So I played with them a bit. I did not want them to feel that I considered them enemies. As a result the townspeople went home with their machetes. They did not cause any trouble, and there is a flourishing congregation there today.

What Do You Translate?

When we were trying to get into Mexico, the officials said No. The man who had said No the strongest was the Director of Rural Education. In 1935 the Lord arranged for specialists to gather in Mexico City for an International Congress. We did not know it, but the Lord got us down there just in time to attend this Congress. After the initial big meeting the Congress divided into groups.

One of the new workers who was with me said, "How much are we going to tell them?"

I said, "I don't know." We walked in the door to attend one of the sessions.

There at the table, with the other delegates to the Congress, was seated the man who had said, "We will not let you translate the Bible, and if you do translate the Bible into the Indian languages, we will not let you distribute it or use it." Immediately, I knew that we had to tell everything, because he already knew.

When I saw him I smiled and reached out my arms to give him an embrace. He got up and embraced me, right there before those delegates. I had forced him to be a friend by showing friendliness. Mexico and Latin America are the realm of friendship. If you can force a man to be a friend, you have won the day.

How does this apply to those of antagonistic religious views? In Peru there were missionaries. Mind you, I love my fellow missionaries, but that does not mean I will follow some of their policies. When policies do not work, when methods do not work, when year after year goes by and the job does not get done, I am going to look for a new method. If carrying a chip on my shoulder does not win an enemy, I am going to get rid of that chip and try to win the foe with love.

Come for Tea.

In Peru there was at least one missionary who would not tip his hat. Now it is a custom to tip your hat to a man in Latin America. But this missionary would not tip his hat to a priest. He would not say Good day to the priest.

That is wrong, he believed. Saying Good day is wishing the priest prosperity. Have a good day. But this man would not do that.

One American priest, who was a Franciscan, said, "After all, we are fellow Americans. At least we could be friendly one to another, couldn't we?" But that man felt that he was compromising if he showed any friendliness to the priest. That attitude, however, does not win the battle. If you can play ping pong with that priest, if you can invite him home for a meal, if you can do him some favor like transport him in your plane, by all means do so. It wets his gun powder and it may win his heart.

One of our couples had gone way back into the jungle of Ecuador on the Aguarico River, where there was a small ethnic group. They got a landing strip started so the plane could bring them in, take them out, and bring supplies. They were winning the confidence of the Indians, when lo and behold here came a Spanish priest and started a mission at the end of their landing strip. What were they going to do?

Mrs. Johnson said, "I know what I am going to do. He will enjoy some good food."

Her husband went to the priest and said, "My wife would like you to come try some of her cooking."

He came once. Then he said, "Listen, we are enemies. I cannot come and eat at your table this way."

"Well, at least come and take tea with us in the afternoon."

"Okay, I will come and take tea with you."

He was a lonely man. The Indians could not talk his language. He wanted a little fellowship, but I suppose he had been ordered by his superior not to be friendly. Well, after he had taken tea a few times, he began remembering that good food he had had.

Mary said, "Won't you come and have a dinner with us?"

"Okay, I'll come." Well, you know, he was able to stick it out for a year and a half or maybe two years. Then he disappeared and the mission was closed down. The last we heard of him he had gone to some place in the Philippines. He was completely whipped by love.

For six years there were seemingly no results. But now the work is going forward, and many are turning to the Lord. They also have a young man who has learned to be a teacher. The Ecuadorian government pays him his salary and they have a school there. Win your enemies by love, or, if you want to put it another way, whip your enemies by love. Lincoln said, "Annihilate your enemies by love." Make them friends. It is all the same thing. It is overcoming evil with good.

Of course, we have our fellow workers and sometimes they can be problems. Try to get together regularly for prayer and Bible reading. Take turns reading the Word. Have a little fellowship service, if you want to. Be patient.

If your fellow worker is talkative and you are not, let him talk and you try to step up your production of talk. One of our girls was talkative; another was not. So they said, "At each meal each one of us will bring a subject of conversation to the table — something we have found in our reading or our studies that morning, or in letters we have received." And it worked! They got along fine.

It is very vital, in getting along with our fellow workers, to always have fellowship around the Word of God and in prayer.

Cameron Townsend

The First Glue

Priorities and Protocol.

I was making instant coffee. It was back in the early days of powdered milk and powdered coffee. And the old-time powdered milk was anything but "instant."

I popped a spoonful of powdered coffee into the cup and a spoonful of powdered milk. Then I poured in the hot water. I proceeded to stir—with diligence and patience. But all I got was a great clot of dumpling-like milk which steadfastly refused to dissolve. "Rats!" I exclaimed in disgust.

"Darling, you've got to put the milk in last," Kay soothed.

"What difference does it make?" I sulked.

"This difference," she explained, pointing to her own creamy-looking cup and my lumpy soup. "Put the milk in first and you get yours; put it in last and you get mine."

It was an important lesson in protocol. Or in ordered rules, if you dislike the word *protocol.*

In the summer of 1945 I was studying under a well-known linguist at a Linguistic Institute in Ann Arbor. Inadvertently I used the word *rule.* "Do not use that word," he remonstrated. "We are writing descriptive, not proscriptive grammars." I was chastened.

It was a big relief when Chomsky brought the word back in. But there was a difference. He was not talking about injunctions or prohibitions but about the sequence in which descriptive statements follow each other. Sometimes a given sequence, like the order in which ingredients are introduced into a cake batter, "works." A different sequence may fail altogether to accomplish its intended purpose.

A good many of us have been raised in environments where very little was required in the way of ordered rules procedures. To be sure, I was expected to comb my hair before breakfast rather than after, and on Christmas morning we were obliged to eat breakfast and have prayers before presents could be opened. But the relative order in which we might meet or call on people seemed always free.

Not so for a foreigner calling on officials in a country whose friendship he hopes to gain. A high official does not appreciate learning from the grape vine that a visitor has arrived and is seeing those under him before seeking to see him.

But high officials are hard to see. How can a person waste time waiting to see the top man when those of lower rank are willing to see him without delay? By making his requests for appointments with the highest men as early as possible. If a man knows his office has been approached first, he can forgive the foreigner for seeing others while waiting for the appointment at the top. And remember that civil officials outrank religious.

Start at the Top.

Isn't the danger of getting a negative reply greater if you start at the highest ranks first? No! Contrary to popular belief, the top man in a hierarchy is not the toughest man. He cannot afford to be.

In fact, he is obligated to be more lenient than those under him because he is the court of last resort. Also, he must strive in any type of government to get maximum credit for achievements, so must be the one saying most of the Yeses. And in a really strict, totalitarian system he is the only one who can say Yes. The lower echelon officials are expected to say No, Wait, Maybe, or I'll ask the boss.

Do not ask for an appointment with a really high official unless you are prepared to wait.

By "really high" we mean a president, cabinet officer or ambassador. It is an insult to such a person to ask for an audience and then tell him you cannot accept the date, several days or a couple of weeks later. If he offers a date, you'd better "break your neck" (meaning break some sacrosanct other plans) to take it. And having accepted, do not postpone or miss it for anything!

In relations with foreign organizations in-country, the state is over the church.

It makes no difference whether it is a united "state-church" society, an American style "no establishment of religion" society or a communist/atheist government. In all cases it is the national government, not a local religious group, which decides whether visas will be issued to representatives of foreign groups.

But you know of groups which got in without approval of the national government? No doubt you do! But it is not the best way. By-passing the national government is a very precarious route for a foreign organization to follow, no matter how warm a reception it may experience from a non-government entity in the country for which entry permission is sought.

It is not the responsibility of a foreigner to decide, in a country not his own, which political group is good and which is bad.

God has repeatedly shown in amazing ways that He can and will use those in power to accomplish His purposes, regardless of the seeming impossibility of any situation. The suffering which Israel endured in Egypt became a powerful deterrent to Satan's attempts to drag them back there. The suffering which they endured in Babylon cured them from the grosser forms of idolatry. Cardenas, who was often called "communist" by American newspapers, gave much personal support to Bible translation in his country.

Do not fancy that the main hope of being allowed to translate in a country lies with the Protestant officials of that country.

Not only the "powers that be" are ordained by God, but also the rank which they hold in the hierarchy. Strict recognition of and adherence to this order must be observed by a foreigner seeking permission for his organization to work in a given country. The temptation to by-pass a higher official because he is a Moslem or Catholic or communist must be resisted at all costs. God has used officials of every imaginable persuasion, functioning in their proper offices, to help His work forward in the way He wants it to go. A Catholic official, for example, in Papua New Guinea, was extremely helpful to the PNG Branch in arrangements for leasing the Ukarumpa property there.

Do not allow members of any SIL unit to make political pronouncements about countries which are not their own.

There is an almost overwhelming tendency, among persons raised in countries where freedom of speech is standard, to exercise the same freedom in countries where they are guests. Even if those are also "free speech" countries, the foreigner simply does not have the right to speak against conditions which he dislikes in such lands.

Do not allow yourself or any member of your organization to give propaganda material to nationals which they can use against friendly officials.

Dr. R. was dismissed as Director of the National School of Anthropology in Mexico for allowing SIL to print Gospel hymns and a few Scripture verses on the school press. In Mexico any such religious activity in a government school is strictly forbidden.

In the foolish years of my student days I kept getting tied in knots by the fanciful dilemmas teachers and other students posed because they made no mention of ordered rules, or the ranking of laws.

"When a stoplight is red but a policeman is standing there waving you to go ahead, which do you do?" It is not a dilemma, because the policeman outranks the stoplight.

"You have heard it said, 'Love your friends and hate your enemies.' But I say, 'Love your enemies'." Which do you do? Love your enemies, because the One Who said that outranks the ones who said the other.

Which came first, the chicken or the egg? It was a problem only because I did not have the sense to identify the individual chicken and the individual egg. Egg X came before chicken Y which was in it. Chicken Y came before egg Z which it laid.

"Is it lawful for us Jews to pay taxes to the unlawful Roman emperor who imposes them?"

"Render to Caesar that which is Caesar's, and to

God that which is God's."

Freedom is very precious indeed. I am more thankful than I can say for the freedom we enjoy. But when I drive up to a Yield sign, I am not free to pull out in front of an approaching car which is not blocked by such a sign. Or, to put it another way, I am free to pour sand into the gas tank instead of gas, but if I do so I will not be free to drive that car very far.

How long should the priority of government relations continue?

I am a teacher of linguistics. And I enjoy teaching linguistics much more than I enjoy doing government relations work. I especially enjoy teaching linguistics to Christians. The enthusiastic response and the warm appreciation make it abundantly worthwhile. The response I get in some government offices, however, is cold, indifferent, unfeeling. No wonder I tend to drift into the teaching of linguistics and out of government relations work!

A similar development took place in one country. Our first contact with a certain government post was very friendly because we greatly needed their help, and we knew it. We were therefore very deferential.

As God prospered the work, our need for their help became less; but a succession of fine Christian people at the post proved easy and delightful to relate to, so relations continued to be excellent.

Then the Christians who loved to help us at the government post left, and a more matter-of-fact officer was appointed. We related to him in a formal way, but little more. His help was not much needed and ours was not much offered, so relations cooled. Then a dunning letter from an SIL department to which a government officer owed money provided a spark which ignited an explosion.

"You SIL people," the officer said, in effect, "love to receive favors but you are not so keen to give them." There followed a long list of good turns the government had done for SIL. "Furthermore," the officer continued, "you like to relate to, and do things for, those of your same religious persuasion, but are slow to help those who differ with you."

Oh, that hurt! Townsend, from the day SIL was founded, had insisted that we must be good neighbors without regard to the religious views of those involved.

But almost certainly the most important point was left unspoken. The people at the post represented the host government. We found it easier and more enjoyable to relate to Christians than to government. The result was understandable: much thought and effort went into Christian relations; much less went into government relations. The priorities which had characterized the beginnings were gradually reversed.

It is not a better way. Government relations must have priority over religious relations not only at the start of a work but also continuously — right up to the end. And the order must be followed not only at the highest levels but also at the lowest. The first man to call on in even the humblest village is the head man, not the pastor. When this is done, both will be content. When it is not done, uneasiness and possible trouble will result.

But God won in the end. The wife of a man from the government post had a baby born at the SIL clinic. The unfeigned love and all-out help of the SIL doctor and nurses made amends for all.

"Man can do anything!" chortled an American official after a successful space mission. He failed to mention that, in order for the astronauts to return safely to earth, they had to re-enter earth's atmosphere with their spaceship in exactly the right attitude, hitting their space-time "window" at exactly the right velocity on the right trajectory. Only as they submitted to the protocol of the laws of physics which governed their space flight could they safely complete it. And it is only as Christians submit to the protocol of the laws of human relations that they can successfully "do anything."

RSP

This Blunt Thing

Whose name is in the bright lights?

Ken Smith and I were calling on the State Secretary of Sabah. We had with us to present to him a copy of the *Tausug-English Dictionary* edited by Irene Hassan, Nurhadan Halud, and Seymour and Lois Ashley. As we presented this beautiful volume, the high official's eyes lit up. "I know how to speak Tausug!" he exclaimed. "My mother is Tausug!"

You can hardly imagine a more propitious beginning for a crucial interview. Some will say, "Oh, yes, we have often given out linguistic works done by our members." But they may be still tragically missing the point. This dictionary's Filipino authors' names not only appear on the cover but also appear first. It is a practice which SIL has sometimes failed to learn and apply. And our hosts overseas are too polite, in most cases, to demur when we fail to display the professional courtesy which can be so vital to our acceptance in the countries where we wish to work.

Some time back the Ambassador of Indonesia to Washington dedicated an International Friendship Helio-Courier plane at Waxhaw for service in Irian Jaya. As I met him for breakfast at the Townsends' that morning, I presented him with a copy of the volume of workshop papers entitled *From Baudi to Indonesian*. As his eyes took in the cover, they lit up. "Suharno," he observed approvingly. "Javanese!"

But it was not the fact that the co-author was from

the same language group as the Ambassador which made the presentation so ideal. It was the fact that Kenneth Pike had put Suharno's name first on the cover and his own name second. Also, the fact that the volume was printed in Indonesia. Cenderawasih University, which serves Irian Jaya and sponsors SIL, gets glory for the volume. Indonesia benefits accordingly, and the Ambassador was delighted.

Getting the names on the front of the cover, however, is still not enough. I was thrilled to see Jean Donaldson's name second on the cover of the White Tai dictionary she co-authored. But it was a terrible shock to see that the publisher had totally omitted the name of the White Tai co-author from the spine.

I used to laugh at fears expressed by some indigenous people that we would "steal" their language. But I finally realized that they had a point. We expatriates are sometimes like the rich man with thousands of sheep who slaughtered his poor neighbor's only lamb to feed his guest. We have thousands of ways of getting recognition. The poor illiterate who has no resource except his knowledge of his own language is not allowed to have first-place cover and title-page recognition for even that, "because we do not do it that way." Instead, we steal the glory, putting our expatriate names either first or alone on cover and title pages of publications featuring the poor man's language.

One of the vast, untapped reservoirs for both good will and linguistic production is to team up linguists, translators and literacy specialists with speakers of indigenous languages and/or national scholars for co-authoring dictionaries, text collections, folklore books, autobiographies of tribal people, flora and fauna books (ethno-botany), primers and readers, geography and history books.

One of the vivid memories I have of India is the anger and bitterness expressed by an Indian scholar toward some expatriates who had worked with Indians in the collection of language data in India and had then used the data for academic degrees and advancement in their home country, with little or no recognition given to the people of India who worked with them.

The Shoshones are one of the North American groups which have been most suspicious of outsiders. When Wes Kosin, working with one of them on a thesaurus, reached the stage of reproducing the book for circulation, he elected to leave his name off the cover and title page entirely, burying it, instead, in the "acknowledgments" section, where the Indian contribution has often been buried. As a result, the thesaurus was very well received. Though there may have been disagreements with orthography or spelling decisions, there was no animosity apparent to the effort as a whole.

Reprint Seed

On one occasion I was "benighted," as the Filipinos say, in Biak. Having considerable time between planes and a good supply of linguistics reprints with me, I decided to seek to meet the district officer. To my delight I discovered that his office was not far from the airport. I was even more pleased when it developed that I could see him after a short wait. We had a pleasant visit. I described our work and gave him a stack of reprints.

Two or three years later it became necessary to call on the Deputy Governor of Irian Jaya in Jayapura. Some decisions were needed, so he brought the Provincial Secretary in on the interview. After going over the business at hand, we relaxed for some pleasantries.

"I have met you before," the secretary averred, "...in Biak." Then I recognized him as the officer I had met in the other district. It was very nice to realize that we were already a long way toward winning his friendship because of the previous visit and reprints given.

When, in 1951, I first visited the Philippines, I met two men with the same surname — Cirio Panganiban and Jose Villa Panganiban. The first was Director of the Institute of National Language and the second was head of the Department of National Language at the University of Santo Tomas. Since they had identical surnames and similar responsibilities, I got them mixed up. Five mailings of reprints intended for Cirio got to Jose Villa instead.

But the Lord knew what He was doing. Cirio passed away not long after we began work in the Philippines, and Jose Villa was appointed to his position shortly after that. Since Jose Villa was a fiery, articulate spokesman for a theological point of view different from ours, there could have been problems, inasmuch as his office was host to ours. But the reprint mailings and subsequent visits had had their effect. Not only was he not hostile to us, he was instead a very faithful friend. Some of us who knew him well and who saw him from time to time during his years of battle with cancer are confident that we will meet him again in heaven. He loved, in those last years, to hear the Scriptures read and to have us lead in prayer. It was a special blessing to read Isaiah 53 to him the last time I saw him before he passed away.

So it hurts to see some of our government relations people be "reprint stingy." I realize that reprints cost money and that we must be good stewards of them. But good stewardship means not only avoidance of waste, but also generous sowing of reprints where the sowing can do the most good. One of the good results is that the reprints accredit us. Much more than calling cards, they inform the recipients who we are and what we do.

Another "good" which they accomplish is to make it plain that we have no intention of being dogs-in-the-manger with language data we get. Since many others refuse to share, our readiness to share is greatly appreciated.

Be Prepared.

All who do either linguistic, literacy or translation work should prepare and carry with them when they go overseas a sheaf of notes to be used in giving linguistic lectures or participating in linguistic seminars. It is not good to plead ignorance or unpreparedness. The very fact that a person has been granted a visa for language work overseas makes it a foregone conclusion that he may be called on for public contributions of his expertise.

There are two excellent reasons for needing to accept public speaking invitations. The first is that linguistic privileges God has given, like all other resources of which He makes people stewards, must be shared with those in host countries. The second is that exposure to public question sessions does much to allay the fears of those who do not understand the work.

Language Planning

Those of us who have been raised in the Bloomfieldian tradition of descriptive linguistics find it difficult to accept some of the current trends in language planning. For most newly independent nations, however, language planning is an inseparable part of the enthusiastic process of nation-building. And some of it is well done. I, for example, could not believe a few years ago that the language planners of Indonesia might succeed in achieving alphabet uniformity with Malaysia. But they did! And it was accomplished with hardly a ripple, considering the magnitude of such a change.

As there is opportunity, therefore, it is very much in order to participate in language planning conferences and seminars. These gatherings, if courteously approached, can achieve great good in terms of vernacular education, spelling agreement, recognition of minority languages, dissipation of language myths, and thawing of animosities between rival linguistic points of view.

Some Booby Traps and Escape Hatches

Part of the naiveté of Westerners doing language study in Asia is due to their ignorance of the dimensions of language loyalties they confront.

Most Westerners, for example, are aware only of flat dialect geography maps which display language boundaries determined by latitude and longitude. In very mountainous places like Nepal, however, certain language groups such as the Sherpas are determined also by altitude.

This, of course, is due in part to occupational and caste factors which may also be present in a completely intermingled group inhabiting a single geographical location. Iron-workers, for example, may speak a dialect quite distinct from that spoken by farmers living in the same village.

Even where there are minimal differences in a spoken language, there may be fierce competing loyalties to different scripts. Compare, for example, the Hindi loyalty to Devanagari and the Urdu loyalty to Arabic script.

And even where there are no differences in the script over a given area, there may be sharply divided allegiances to two or more different spelling traditions as in some parts of South India.

Perhaps the most troublesome of all is the fact that differing lexical values may be assigned to a given word in different places. Some linguists are gravely remiss in continuing to use the word *informant* to describe those who teach their languages. Even in North America a majority of the people who hear that word interpret it as synonymous with *informer*.

How does one who wants to be helpful thread his way through such a maze of antipathies? There is no single easy way, but there are some good guidelines which are helpful almost everywhere.

The first is to try to keep all options open. The temptation to side "against" any option can be a bad trap and may cost a person his acceptance with a given group.

The second is to seek to learn the good points of each option; Arabic script, for example, is more attractive than Roman, but Roman is easier to type. One may be more prestigious than a second, but the second more economical than the first. One may be more ancient; sometimes, however, there are good reasons to prefer a more modern. In any given group and in any given discussion it is important to be able to recognize these values and not belittle them.

Sometimes it is possible to embrace more than one option successfully. Some schools, for example, claim good results in starting children on an "initial teaching alphabet" which permits them to read without the irregularities of the historical spelling conventions of their national language. Those who go on to higher education then learn the standard patterns in due course. The military in Pakistan, we are told, introduce illiterate recruits to written Urdu in a Romanized spelling first. They go on to learn Arabic script later.

It is important to remember that what is regarded as "conservative" in one time or place was or will be viewed as "radical" in another. A restrained and courteous attitude toward both radicalism and conservatism in linguistic matters may be important. This is not the same as lukewarmism, however.

Shall we trade off the SIL birthright?

For fifteen years I sought permission for SIL to work in a certain country. During much of that time friends were urging that we not go in as SIL under the Ministry of Education but as missionaries sponsored by churches who would seek visa authorization from the Minister of Religion. The second route was being successfully followed by others. Why delay start of the work in an attempt to proceed under another Ministry?

One day, several years after our attempts to go the first route had finally succeeded, a government decree was published giving missionaries just two years to hand their work over to nationals and leave. In consternation some asked what the decree would do to our work. "Not a thing," I replied, "as far as I can tell. That decree was put out by the Ministry of Religion and our work is under the Ministry of Education."

One of the priceless birthrights which God has given to the Summer Institute of Linguistics is an identity which is now recognized world-wide. Yet some, for limited local or temporal advantage, would be willing to trade this invaluable inheritance and take some religious or denominational tag in its place. This is perhaps felt with special attraction by persons who do not consider themselves linguists and who, therefore, have difficulty adjusting to a linguistic label.

But a religious or denominational label would not be easier. Our pilots, mechanics, and radio men are no more translators than they are linguists. Our Baptists would not feel easier if they were regarded as Presbyterians, nor our Presbyterians if they were regarded as Baptists. And the overwhelming majority of the membership has never been accredited to perform marriages, funerals, or administration of the Lord's Supper in the official manner recognized by most denominations. To take on an organizational or church member image, therefore, which would lead more people to assume that we are so accredited, would be far more misleading than the SIL image.

My undergraduate major was history. One of the strong impressions lingering with me from my readings in history is that of endless wars the world has been through for religious control of the lives of men. And although we who are "enlightened" feel that we would never let ourselves be drawn into such a war, the on-going death toll in places like Northern Ireland and Lebanon is a reminder that inflamed religious sentiments are not entirely things of the past. If we insist on leading with a foot called "Protestant," or even with a foot called "Christian," we could very well, in many countries, antagonize immediately the very people God has called us to serve.

And our closest Christian and missionary friends themselves can cooperate more easily with us if we have a "neutral" quality than they can if we have an image which savors of religious competition with their groups. Mr. Townsend, in his work overseas, was very careful to avoid identification with any single religious group so that he could more effectively serve all. He never allowed himself to be called "Reverend," nor to be viewed as the "Pastor" of any church.

If there was any verse which Mr. Townsend quoted more than any other in letters written to communicate our vision, it was Romans 15:20. Surely, when the Lord has provided such wonderful foundations of our own to build on, we should do so!

OPPORTUNITY

This I beheld, or dreamed it in a dream:
There spread a cloud of dust along a plain;
And underneath the cloud, or in it, raged
A furious battle, and men yelled, and swords
Shocked upon swords and shields. A prince's banner
Wavered, then staggered backward, hemmed by foes.

A craven hung along the battle's edge,
And thought, "Had I a sword of keener steel —
That blue blade that the king's son bears — but this
Blunt thing!" — he snapped and flung it from his hand.
And lowering crept away and left the field.

Then came the king's son, wounded, sore bestead,
And weaponless, and saw the broken sword,
Hilt-buried in the dry and trodden sand,
And ran and snatched it, and with battle-shout
Lifted afresh he hewed his enemy down,
And saved a great cause that heroic day.

— Edward R. Sill

RSP

Sixteen Ways to Help
Stay in Business

1. Entertain educational and other officials at dinners, teas, or some functions of special interest.

2. Consult educators and officials often, at least every six months, about plans, problems, etc.

3. Report to officials regularly. Annually, the report could be in writing.

4. Ask officials for help on worthy projects and give them the main credit for accomplishments.

5. Introduce all new recruits to educators, anthropologists, etc. when they first arrive in the country from abroad.

6. Join local scientific societies if possible, or at least attend their open sessions.

7. Attend lectures given or organized by officials and educators.

8. Offer the educational department or universities display materials from time to time.

9. When one of our linguists comes to the city with interesting linguistic or educational developments or findings to report, set up a meeting with some government educator or anthropologist who might be interested.

10. Publish articles in local publications, both scientific and popular.

11. Have a national sponsoring committee with the

President and the Minister of Education as honorary president and vice-president.

12. Find some basis for a contract with some government agency every two or three years. One reason for a contract would be literacy or bilingual education, publications and research programs.

13. Read carefully Ben Elson's article in this book — "The Basic Distinctive of SIL."

14. Do not accept invitations to preach or hold office in city churches.

15. Avoid participation in ecclesiastical meetings, conferences, etc.

16. Place no restrictions on nationals who want to translate the Bible.

Cameron Townsend
December 1974

The SIL Program
and Flexibility

For many, perhaps most, of our members, the SIL program consists of a package: language learning and analysis, including publishing the results of the analysis, devising a practical alphabet, constructing primers and teaching literacy or becoming involved in a bilingual education program, doing a bit of community development work or serving the village where we work in some way, and finally translating the New Testament.

It is often felt that this "package" was developed by Uncle Cam in 1935 when he and others with him first went to Mexico. It also seems to be assumed that this package is taken to government officials in countries where we would like to work, inspected by them and either bought or not as a whole. Part of the package includes the notion that it will be carried out by foreigners, who will need aircraft and radio support in doing the work. The package is rather rigidly conceived and stands or falls pretty much as a whole.

In some debates it is asserted that the package was fine for 1935 and many years after, but that the world has changed and it will not work today. We must therefore develop new and more flexible approaches.

The thesis of this essay is that (1) I do not believe Uncle Cam had a package he wanted to sell in 1935 or subsequently but (2) the package was developed by others of us who felt it was just what the countries and the minority groups needed. I believe we, not Uncle Cam, made it rigid.

Uncle Cam, I believe, had a goal and three operating principles. I do not believe that he had the kind of clear-cut "package" we see as the SIL program today. First, he had a goal — to translate the New Testament for the Indian peoples of Mexico (and elsewhere). Then, he had three operating principles: (1) service to all because of Christ's love; (2) keeping the government informed of our whereabouts and activities; and (3) close identification with the people and nations.

I have heard Uncle Cam and others say that when they went to Mexico in 1935 they were willing to dig ditches, if by doing so they could translate the Scriptures for the Indians. As it turned out ditch digging was unnecessary. We could be students of Indian languages. But the flexibility of being ditch diggers if necessary was there. The heavy academic interest in linguistics and literacy is a later development and has become part of the "package." To a degree these things have become ends in themselves, a situation which makes the "package" more rigid. Perhaps we need to get back to the position that we are willing to do anything (dig ditches) to see the goal of translating the Scriptures accomplished.

What I am trying to say is that I believe we have gotten away from the original flexibility that Uncle Cam had. I believe for the most part we have gotten away from his operating principles as well.

Let me try to illustrate what I mean a little more. Uncle Cam's first operating principle is *service to all*. When he first went to Mexico he did two things as he tried to figure out ways to serve the government and the people where he personally was allocated. It was not particularly easy to serve the government, but he took various kinds of initiatives. First, he consulted with both government officials and scholars about which Indian languages they would like studied, and allocations were made in accord with their interest and recommendations. Second, among the Aztecs where he located, he began to make a garden for the people; he later interested the government in putting in a water system, which he helped with, and in planting a grove of orange trees for the village as a communal project. He also tried to serve in other ways, which will be mentioned below.

When he went to South America (Peru, first) he continued to demonstrate the service-to-all principle by insisting that our planes fly not only government officials as needed, but also Catholic missionaries in the jungle area. Christ's love extends to all; therefore our service should be to all.

As a part of the service to the government, the bilingual school system was begun. If I understand Uncle Cam correctly, this system was not set up as a model for all fields, or as a part of the SIL package, but as an act of service to the government which he felt was needed at the time. It was service both to the government and to the Indian peoples.

The second principle Uncle Cam followed very carefully was keeping the relevant government officials informed of our activities. Often he told me, "Call on officials whether you need anything or not. Then if they have questions, they can ask you, rather than having to call you in." Not only should we call on them in their official capacities, but also entertain them in our homes. Let them get to know us. Live in a glass house, as far as officials are concerned. We are guests in their country. We should treat them with friendliness, honor, and courtesy.

Finally, it has been Uncle Cam's belief that we

should identify with the people we are working with and with the country. He showed this identification in Mexico in the early days in various ways. One way was his biography of President Cardenas. In it he spoke positively of the President and the achievements of the nation. Another way was identifying with the Mexican point of view when the Mexican government expropriated the holdings of the large oil companies in the late 30's. He asked President Cardenas if he would object if he (Uncle Cam) went on a speaking tour in the U.S. to explain to the American people the Mexican point of view in the controversy. He also wrote a booklet *The Truth about Mexico's Oil,* which defended the Mexico government's point of view. He also wrote an article on the rural educational system in Mexico which was published in the States.

Many of us find this kind of identification very hard to achieve. I cite the above to show the extent to which Uncle Cam believed in identification. He also tried to get us to understand the need to identify by being friendly and hospitable. When he was around in Mexico there were always dinners for officials, and during these times we all had opportunity to show our identification with the nation in various ways. The dinners were opportunities to do just that.

Within the limits of our goal and these operating principles, I believe Uncle Cam was exceedingly flexible. The Friendship Fleet of planes was an attempt to bring the Latin American nations to the attention of the American people. Giving the planes to the government of the country for our use was risky, but it demonstrated that we wanted to serve and that we trusted them to take care of us. Very few of us come up with that kind of flexibility.

I think that we need to carefully examine our programs and see if we have the goal in focus and the operating principles straight. It seems to me hard to imagine a more flexible approach than Uncle Cam demonstrated. If it has become rigid it is the fault of some of the rest of us who thought we knew better how things should be done.

Ben Elson
Reprinted from
September 1976 *INTERCOM*

The Basic Distinctive of SIL

For years, as a member of SIL, I did not fully understand SIL. I assumed, incorrectly, the following:

1. "The basic distinctive of SIL is that it is a *linguistic research organization* whose members also engage in literacy and Bible translation."

Although much of the above statement is true, I think it is basically incorrect because of the words *basic distinctive*. Yet I suspect the great majority of our members would agree with it. But, I now believe, those who agree with the above statement have not heard what our founder has been saying all these years. I have now come to what I believe is the correct understanding of SIL:

2. "The basic distinctive of SIL is that it is a nonsectarian (nonreligious) organization whose reporting relationship in the countries where we work is to the national government."

Please observe that I am talking about the *fundamental distinctive*. Perhaps I should not state the case so strongly but say "among the fundamental distinctives." This would also include #1. But, I believe, we must not omit #2.

If our fundamental distinctive is a nonreligious (linguistics) organization whose reporting relationship is to host governments, this precludes many relationships that at first blush seem okay.

Let me now try to justify the assertion that the second statement is the historically correct one. I believe that Article II, Purpose, of the Mexico Branch constitution goes back to the very beginning and has never been significantly revised. So far as I know, it was the first formal document ever devised. Part (b) reads, "To seek to carry out its linguistic investigations in cooperation with the government agencies of the Republic of Mexico and such organizations as pursue related objectives to those of the Branch."

This seems like a strange statement in an Article of Purpose, unless it reflects something basically significant. I conclude from this that it is part of our *basic purpose* to relate to the national government.

The second bit of evidence is the way Uncle Cam has talked to us over the past 40 years of our existence. His talks and messages have almost always been on the blessings and helpfulness of close contact with government officials, and warnings not to stray from our God-given methods. I believe in his mind the fundamental method is relating to the government.

The third bit of evidence again goes back to history. I have heard Uncle Cam, Ken Pike and other early members say, "We were willing to dig ditches, if this would allow us to translate the Scriptures for the Indians." Note here the emphasis is not on linguistics but upon (almost) any (governmental) relationship that would permit them to be in the country and do the translation. God allowed linguistics to be the key and to grow and develop, but underlying that is the government relationship.

I will concede that this fundamental principle has not always been clearly articulated, but I believe that careful looking at the evidence will show it to be there.

If we look at "flexibility" in terms of, or in the context of, statement #1, I can see that almost any kind of church-related activity or relationship is possible. On the other hand, if we talk about "flexibility" in terms of statement #2, then we have a very different situation indeed.

Again, if we look at history, I believe that within the context of statement #2, we have been quite flexible. In Mexico, especially until the mid-50's and perhaps after, our primary emphasis was upon linguistic investigation and linguistic scholarship, including publication. Linguistic scholars were developed by being sent on to grad school – Pike, Nida, Wonderly, Pittman, Gudschinsky, Longacre, to name most of the early ones. In Peru, on the other hand, the primary emphasis for a long time during the early years was on bilingual schools. I believe the two branches developed very differently, in response to different situations.

It has been rumored that Uncle Cam's thinking really matured in Peru, and that the Peru way is how things should really be done. I once asked Uncle Cam if this were true. He indicated that it was not. The bilingual schools, he affirmed, were started in response to the specific situation in Peru which was different from that in Mexico or elsewhere. He was being flexible within the context of statement #2, and that was the result.

At a board meeting in Dallas some years ago, Bernie May stated that, in his opinion, our people did not know who they were. I think the reason is that we have begun to lose sight of our most basic distinctive.

When we begin to move from fundamental distinctive without telling ourselves what we are doing, there is a feeling of considerable unease. It is this, I think, that accounts for members' concern about polarization on matters of strategy. We must decide clearly who we are before we can decide what flexibility means.

Ben Elson

Why Would the Government Want Us to Stay?

In a recent discussion with Jerry Elder and Bob Gunn the question came up, "Why does the government want us to stay in the country anyway?" It is a key question. The more I thought about it, the more I realized the answer is fundamental to our whole being. I asked Dick Pittman for his thoughts and he wrote up the following which I am glad to share with you:

Why would the government of _____ want us to stay?

1. For the benefit of national anthropologists. Every anthropologist needs the vast linguistic resources of the ethnic group he studies, but few can take the time to make these available in published form as is done by the Summer Institute of Linguistics. Dictionaries, grammars, and phonological studies are tedious and expensive to prepare, but they are gold mines of reference information and an absolute necessity for any anthropologist who would do thorough work regarding any community.

2. For the benefit of national educators. The government of _____ is committed to giving the best possible education to its ethnic minorities, and it recognizes the importance of taking the mother tongue of the learner into account in teaching anyone to read. It is not possible, however, to take the mother tongue into account unless and until thorough studies of the mother tongue have been made and published so as to be availa-

ble to the educators who are responsible for teaching the people in question.

3. For the benefit of the Department of Health. As in the case of education, the government is committed to protecting the health of its citizens. Not infrequently, however, misunderstandings arise between language groups and doctors because the presuppositions and vocabulary of ethnomedicine and those of modern national medicine are different. It is not possible to require doctors and nurses to master indigenous languages as a prerequisite to their service to the people. It is possible, however, to expect SIL reference books on indigenous languages to be added to the "kit of instruments" these doctors and nurses use to give best possible service to these people.

4. For the benefit of the Department of Agriculture. _____, like several other parts of the Western Hemisphere, is the place of origin of numerous varieties of food and medicinal plants which have benefited the entire world. The cultural minorities, through trial and error over the centuries, have discovered the use and value of these plants and the manner of cultivating them.

The Aztec Indians of Mexico, for example, know how to use a local herb to help keep their turkeys healthy. Since turkey raising is increasing in many parts of the world, knowledge of the beneficial value of this herb is also of great value.

5. For the preservation of the cultural patrimony of _____. It is not overly difficult for photographers to capture with cameras and tape recorders some of the music and dances of the people. But to record and preserve the folklore, history, philosophy, world view, ethnobotany, and scores of other aspects of culture which are enshrined in language is a work requiring thousands

of man-hours by hundreds of linguists, both national and foreign. Even if SIL continues for another ten years, the surface will barely be scratched. The resources remaining for national scholars to study will still be vast. But if present studies are stopped, some of the priceless cultural data will be lost forever.

6. To ensure affectionate rapport between the government of _____ and its cultural minorities. All the great empires of history foundered on the reef of misunderstanding between the conquerors and the conquered, partly because there was a language difference and partly because the conquerors ridiculed and insulted the languages and cultures of the conquered.

But the dissolution of empires and the transfer of authority to the descendants of the conquerors born on the conquered soil has not ended the problem. The lack of appreciation because of not understanding intricacies of language often continues to this day.

As research into the languages and cultures continues, however, and as the growing weight of documentation increasingly generates respect for the beautiful, eloquent and powerful resources of the ethnic languages, government becomes admiring of its people, and the people develop self-confidence instead of hopelessness. The result is mutual respect and esteem instead of mutual distrust.

It is instructive, in this respect, to study the Basques of Spain and those of France. In Spain they were prohibited from putting Basque signs over their shops and Basque inscriptions on their tombstones. In France they were not only free to do so, but even to found a Basque University with as many courses taught in the Basque language as they could possibly desire. When the Basque separatists of Spain tried to get the Basques of France to make common cause with them, the French Basques said, "Why? We love France. We are proud to be citizens of a country which honors our language in this way."

7. For the benefit of the ethnic groups of _____. Even when all possible national and foreign assistance has been given to enable these people to reach their highest potential, much will still remain to be done. If _____ allows SIL to stay, however, and if _____ also seeks by every human and educational means possible to provide optimal conditions for the people to make enlightened choices and to build well on these choices, neither the cultural minorities nor the government need ever say, "It was an ill wind which brought us together."

Bernie May

Who Reports to Whom?

"And remember, if anything goes sour with our relationship, my head will roll, not yours." It was the head of a university talking to us. He had stuck out his neck to sign the agreement sponsoring us. From our point of view he was getting a good thing. But from his point of view he was taking a big risk. And he was right.

Years ago the head of a large school similar to his allowed us to use the school press to print a hymn book in an Indian language. In the process we also ran off two or three verses of Scripture on the same press. One day, to my consternation, the noon edition of a major metropolitan daily appeared with a headline screaming across all eight columns of its front page, "In the Department of Education they are printing Gospels in Indian languages." This was not complimentary. The country had strict laws requiring total separation of religious activities from public schools.

By suppertime that day, the school official had been fired from his position. When I first began to work with other expatriates in a country not our own, I took it for granted that the reporting relationship was up through the ranks from one expatriate to another until the reports finally wound up on desks of those over us back home. Only slowly did I tumble to the fact that, if we wanted to continue living and working in the country in question, our reports had to be written for, and end up on, the desk of the sponsoring official in the land to which we had come.

In this connection, it is of very great importance to remember that every person in public service has rivals who seek by one means or another to unseat those in office. And it often happens that expatriates unwittingly make statements, orally or in writing, which persons out of office can use to unseat persons in office. However true or well-motivated these statements may be, it is very wrong for a person to make statements which can be used against his sponsor.

It is in order, at this point, to mention a curious perversion of the ninth commandment. God said, "Thou shalt not bear false witness." This has been changed in our day to "Thou shalt be honest." One reason, no doubt, is that the second is put in a positive way, and so seems better than the first, which is one of the difficult "thou shalt not's." But the practical outworking of the "thou shalt be honest" command is that a person is led to believe that "honesty" requires him to say all he knows and whatever he thinks. It is as though nakedness were put forward as essential in public because the wearing of clothing conceals something.

Throughout Asia, including Arabic Asia, there is a strong tradition that a man who has given food and shelter to a stranger must then defend and protect him against attack. I have not heard it verbalized, but the converse must surely be at least as binding: a person who has accepted the hospitality of another must not, under any circumstances, contribute to the downfall of the one who gave him food and shelter. Loyalty is even more binding on a Christian than on non-Christians.

It is obvious that the expatriate organization overseas is ultimately responsible to the host government in the country where the organization works. But unless some officer overseas reports to the sponsoring national officer, the director of the branch working there must be the one.

RSP

They Never Give
Me a Report

I was reading a critical newspaper article. The target of the criticism was SIL, so my reaction was mixed — rejecting much of what I read because I knew it to be untrue, but watching warily for a shoe which might fit and therefore have to be put on.

Suddenly I caught a fatal phrase. The reporter quoted a high government official as saying, "I do not know what SIL does. They never give me a report."

I had no idea whether the reporter and/or official were telling the truth or not. But I did know that if this detail were true, someone in SIL had been very remiss. A written report, at least once a year, designed to be read by all of the officials who are most responsible for us, is a must for every country in which SIL works.

Lest this seem too much to ask, I would hasten to add that there is no reason why it should be an expensive, illustrated, book-like production. A neat mimeographed piece without pictures is entirely adequate. In fact, there are some serious considerations for *not* using pictures. Pictures of expatriates can give a wrong or undesirable impression. Certainly they invite comparisons which can easily be invidious. Also typographical errors are more easily forgiven in a pictureless, mimeographed report than they are in an expensive, glossy paper effort.

There is also a temptation to substitute an expensive annual report for serious publication of carefully done linguistic books and articles. This should be resisted. Fine linguistic production is our best credential, not an elaborate report of our work.

Should the report include a listing of hymnbooks and Scripture publications printed during the year in question? No. For several reasons:

1. Every government, whether secular or church-related, is responsible to its citizens to be even-handed in dealing with competing religious systems, including those which reject religion. The translation of documents which are perceived as religious, therefore, is a highly sensitive issue, especially when it is done by expatriates. Admittedly some countries have allowed such translation to be specifically identified in contracts which they have signed, but if we then say, "The government contracted for us to translate New Testaments," we put the government in a difficult position. In the strictest sense they did not contract for us to translate New Testaments. They contracted for us to do technical, non-religious work which could benefit their citizens of all persuasions. The translation was permitted because of our urging.

2. Inclusion of "religious" material in an annual report invites possibly awkward comparison with linguistic and literacy material published during the same time.

3. The importance of being accountable for man hours spent in the host country may seem to be satisfied by a large volume of translation published, and this may salve the conscience for not doing "practical" projects. But every host country wants to see a substantial output of project effort which all citizens recognize as being of "practical" benefit to the country. Unless a branch is struggling to keep up its output of such contributions, it may lose its acceptability with its host.

Does that mean the translation should be hidden?

No. The beautiful, effective way to report it is by inviting officials to the dedications of New Testaments, presenting copies to high officials in personal visits, telling stirring stories of the effects of the translations on those who have read them. Uncle Cam presented a copy of his Cakchiquel New Testament years ago to the President of Guatemala. When a Cakchiquel came to the President protesting something or someone, the President produced it and urged him to read it. He could not have done so if all he had was a report which told of the translation.

Should the annual report to a host government include a financial statement? The problem is that SIL members are volunteers, reponsible for their own support. The organization is not in a position, therefore, to give a complete financial report for all its members to a host government. If the host government or a funding agency expects a financial report of a specific project, that should be done in the way expected in a report devoted to that project.

How about the long lists of names of expatriates? Some government offices (e.g., immigration) may routinely request or expect such lists. Others may be annoyed by them. It seems wise in such cases to prepare lists as addenda or supplements to the annual report and present them only to those offices which need to be kept informed.

Is there a way to reconcile the need to give glory to those with whom we work, while admitting our responsibility for the work we are doing? Definitely. When highly commendable successes have been achieved, names of nationals, individuals in cultural minorities, should be given maximum credit if at all possible. Names of expatriates should be featured much less, except where ultimate responsibility must be assigned. Far more authorship credit should be given to tribal authors for work on dictionary and folklore materials than has been done in the past.

Can written reports be a substitute for personal visits? Not really. Even a written report should be hand-carried, if at all possible, to each official for whom a copy is intended, and a friendly conversation should be developed around it. What better excuse for calling on the one who said, "They never give me a report."

RSP

Every Tub Shall Stand
on Its Own Bottom

It May Be Easier, But...

There are a good many SIL people who, basing their decisions on background experience in their home country, or on the advice of missionaries or of national Christians, figure that the best and fastest way to get started in any country is to go through the good offices of missionaries who have been there longer, or through Christian government officials, or through national church leaders. But this is a temptation which must be resisted. Since government officials are *always* over religious officials when it comes to dealing with foreigners, it is essential to go to the government officials first. And SIL work normally comes under the Minister of Education. So he should be looked to for decisions and leadership whether he is a Christian or not. Take the case of Vietnam, for example:

You could not ask for more kindness than was shown to Ben and Hilda Needham by the Christian and Missionary Alliance when the Needhams visited Vietnam in 1955. Furthermore, they were assured that if SIL decided to work in Vietnam, the C&MA would do everything they could to help.

No one knew better than I that we needed help. I had gone through deep waters seeking permission for us to work in the Philippines. I was contemplating Vietnam from a bed in a Manila hospital where a ruptured appendix had laid me low. From another room in the same hospital continual SOS signals were being sent out for Christians and missionaries to donate blood for Myra Lou Barnard, whose shocking burns had her hovering between life and death.

So why not ask C&MA to run interference for us in Vietnam? I could have done so. But God had given *us* resources, too. President Magsaysay knew President Diem and was willing to give me a letter of introduction. The Philippine Ambassador in Saigon was prepared, on the strength of that letter, to recommend a hotel for me to stay in and to send his consul to the airport to meet me.

When I returned to Saigon in December 1957 with Dave Thomas, we enjoyed the additional asset of having become acquainted with the Rector of the University of Saigon and one of his influential faculty members at the Pacific Science Congress in Bangkok just before. And the former Dean of the Graduate School of the University of North Dakota, together with his wife, was prepared to take us into their home for the first few days after our arrival in Saigon.

But would it not have been better to have accepted the hospitality offered at the C&MA guest house and the savoir faire of their government relations man? No. Going the route that we did, though it seemed harder at first, got us farther in the end. The day came, in fact, when the Minister of Interior told me that we were the only foreigners whom he was allowing to live in villages. And the immigration officials gave us exceptionally kind treatment because we were teaching them English.

Singapore is another case in point. We have had Christian friends there for years, especially with OMF. Their hospitality was always extended to us, and in the days before we were prepared to propose any work there,

I often accepted it. However, when Yu-hung and Pi-lien Chang, after finding the Lord at North Dakota SIL, took a position teaching linguistics at the University of Singapore, and when, in a very providential way, it became clear that they wanted me to stay with them whenever I passed through Singapore, I made that my Singapore "home."

OMF and the Singapore Bible College, I am sure, as well as a young Chinese evangelist to whom I had been introduced, would have been willing to introduce us to government officials — perhaps even to seek documentation for us. But God had something better in store. In February 1976 Secretary of Education Manuel, of the Philippines, gave me a letter of introduction to the Senior Minister of State for Education of Singapore. This gentleman, who is Chinese, referred me to the Director of the Regional Language Centre, who was also Chinese. Since Yu-hung had worked for her, he accompanied me. The relations with all three of these fine Chinese people are our own, not borrowed or reflected ones.

Of course, cultivating the friendship of government officials *before* talking to Christians in any given country is by far the harder route to go. But it is also by far the best route to go. In many cases it is, in fact, the only route which, consistently followed, will result in continuing residence in the country in question.

See Officials First.

I cannot remember who introduced me to the Sultan of Jogjakarta. But I am sure it was not an American. And I do know that it took a fair bit of effort for me, on my first trip to Indonesia, to get to Jogjakarta to meet him. Because we seemed to have so little in common, it would have been easy to give up later attempts to call on him. But God gave grace to keep the contact alive. After several visits to Indonesia I arrived again to find that he had become Vice President. I feared he might now be too busy to see me. But to my surprise he continued to grant interviews as often as possible. As I described our linguistics and Bible translation on one such visit, he said, "Irian Jaya is the place where there is still scope for your work." His views were no doubt a part of the total government decision package on SIL in Indonesia.

When Dr. Cecilio Lopez of the Philippines introduced me to the Indonesian linguist Prijono, the latter was Dean of the Faculty of Letters of the University of Indonesia. He received me kindly, however, and I was able to interact with him in a mutually enjoyable way on linguistic matters. Before long he became Minister of Elementary Education. Even in this much busier role he was happy to see me and gave me unhurried interviews.

One day I arrived to find he was in the hospital. With little hope that I would be allowed to see him I went and, to my surprise, was not only ushered immediately in, but found him sitting up and happy to see me. After small talk on various subjects I presented a Gospel of John in one of the modern English versions. (He handled English very well.) "I have English, Dutch and Javanese Bibles by my bed," he said. "I often read a chapter before I go to sleep. What do you recommend I read in John?"

"Chapters three and fourteen are two of my favorites," I replied. He opened the Gospel and immediately began to read. He was still reading when I left. God took him (to heaven, I believe) not long afterwards.

The first time I met Carlos Romulo was in 1951. He was already Minister of Foreign Affairs at that time. As on so many other occasions, I could hardly believe that a busy cabinet officer would consent to see me. But I was allowed to see him without an appointment, and after only 15 minutes' wait. Faithful continuing contacts, not only by myself but also by Mr. Townsend and several of the Philippine Branch Directors and JAARS officers, resulted in his ultimately becoming Honorary Chairman of the SIL Advisory Committee in the Philippines and giving much help, including introductions to officials in several other Asian countries.

When I first met Ramon Magsaysay he was Secretary of Defense. At that time we did not have a JAARS program, so there seemed little point in making on-going efforts to see him. But God enabled us to resist the temptation to neglect calling on him. Kay and Bobie McKaughan's delicious pineapple and papaya jam gave a fine opportunity to call on Mrs. Magsaysay. Miraculously I was able to see RM twice in the hospital and give Bible verses to encourage him.

Some would seek to load SIL leaders with so many responsibilities that they cannot keep in close touch with men like the above. But making and keeping such friendships is imperative.

Who Can Suffer?

This leads to one of the hardest questions of all: Most management technique depends heavily on vertical reporting relationships through the (expatriate) management hierarchy, and leaves essentially no room for reporting to officials of the host country. Or if there is, it is tacked on as a necessary step, to be used only as much as is minimally required. But there is a deep and subtle danger in that view. Unless an organization learns, overseas, that its lifeline reporting relationship in a given country is to the official responsible for it there, it may not last long in that country. Consider, for example, what an early sponsor said to me in Indonesia: "Remember, if anything goes sour with our relationship, it is I who will suffer, not you."

The firing of our sponsor, a high education official in another country, because of an indiscretion on our part made vividly clear that the Indonesian educator was exactly right. Every SIL member in any country in which SIL works is responsible to try to put officials of the host government in a good light and to avoid words or actions which could be used by political opponents to injure our hosts. Who can suffer? They can!

RSP

To Write
or Not to Write

The cult of "honesty" (tell all) makes us feel it important not only to write negative feelings toward certain people but also to record our irritation with the country we live in, interviews we have had, and people we rub elbows with.

There may be some therapeutic or safety-valve value in doing this at certain times or places, especially in "speaking the truth in love," face-to-face and alone, to one with whom we disagree. In fact, there are strong exhortations in the Bible to do just that. (Mt. 5:23,24;18:15). But committing the criticism to writing, either to the adversary or about an adversary you identify, is something else. In most cases it should *not* be done.

On my first visit to the Philippines I was given a very useful list of the languages of the Philippines which included, along with language data, a critical comment about a veteran missionary. The writer, of course, never intended that the missionary should see the comment. And I forgot all about the comment until, as I was visiting the missionary and mentioned the list, he asked if he might see it. I produced it, handed it over, then watched in shock as he winced at the criticism written against him. I later learned that the criticism was only hearsay and had very little basis in fact. I came to admire the veteran very much. How I wished I had never shown him the language list, and how the writer of the comment wished the comment had never been written!

Early in the days of the Peace Corps, a Peace Corps worker in Africa wrote a postcard home with some uncomplimentary remarks about the country in which she was working. The card was read by postal employees in the host country, shown to higher authorities, and created such a disturbance as to greatly harm and hinder the Peace Corps work in that place.

So how can a person communicate his concerns, misgivings and warnings? In cases where it is a host country or citizens of the host country who are likely to be mentioned, do *not* do it in writing. In most cases, in fact, it is better not to verbalize criticisms at all.

"A bird," warned Solomon (Eccl. 10:20), "will carry the voice, and that which hath wings will tell the matter."

                                                    RSP

Why Not Go to the Ministry First?

How Radio and Aviation Began in One Host Country

We went to the Ministry of Education, who are our hosts, and told them that we would like to make available to them our equipment and expertise in radio. They were delighted. The Minister of Education jumped up from behind his desk. He went around to a map and began putting his finger on places. "This is a school," he said, "where, during the wet season, we do not have any communication for six months. If we had a radio there, I could keep informed of their problems. I could help supply their needs."

He indicated another place and said, "This is the school I went to. I have a special interest in this school, but I cannot keep staff there. They say it is too remote. If we could have an airstrip there and a radio, maybe I could keep teachers at that school. I've got a problem. After teachers get some education they do not want to live in these isolated places. I may have to close my alma mater, the school I graduated from, because I cannot keep my staff there." He was enthusiastic about our proposal.

We then faced the problem of building a radio shop. We were all prepared to construct a building, but someone suggested, "Why don't you go first to the Ministry, tell them the equipment is arriving, and ask them where they would like you to put it?" So we did that. We went to them and said, "The test equipment has come and the first 13 radios have arrived." This time the Director of Education, the highest civil servant in the Ministry, got up from his desk, walked to the door, and gave some orders to his staff members. Bill Sasnett and I were then escorted all over the Ministry of Education headquarters building. We were taken to every office except the Minister's office. Our guide would open a door to an office full of people working, typewriters clacking, and business going on. Then he would say, "Would you like this one?" We were a little embarrassed. I think we could have said, "The second story of this building will be fine," and he would have started moving the desks out. We finally settled for a storeroom which is under the Director's office. It has an outside access next to it. They said, "Fine. Move all the stored stuff out." They moved all the goods out of the storeroom and found another place for it. For a while they stacked it in the halls. Then Bill Sasnett moved his radio equipment in.

That radio equipment now is being used by the Ministry of Education. Whenever we need a radio in the bush, we make every attempt to place it in a Ministry of Education facility. Some of our people have to walk to the nearest school to use the radio. They do not have it in their houses. The radio operator is a school official. This has resulted in the Ministry of Education's being proud of their communication system.

Periodically the Minister or the Director will open the door and usher in, for example, the Minister of Agriculture. The Minister of Education will say, "I want you to see our radios." As Bill shows him around, the Minister offers the use of the radios to the other government official; and he is delighted with the facility which we have helped create for them.

There is no suspicion of the radios. Or if there is suspicion, it is settled within government circles. If one of the local army commanders wonders why there is a radio out there, the local school officials answer. We are not the ones to answer. We do not have to apologize. We do not have to explain that we have permission from the government and produce a letter signed in the capital. We simply say, "Would you mind talking to the Headmaster? It is his radio." Then the army man and a local man sit down together and talk about it. If there are any further questions, they are not addressed to the SIL Director. He is not called down to the army base and told, "We want you to explain yourself." The questioners talk to the Minister of Education and his staff. And the arrangement is working out to be a real blessing. It has increased our effectiveness in the country.

And the same thing applies to the airplane. The airplane is a Ministry of Education/SIL airplane. Other government officials borrow it from the Ministry of Education, not from us. We try to make this clear when the airplane is being used. We try not to exploit the PR value of it for ourselves but very proudly say, "This is the Ministry's airplane. The Ministry operates it. We work for the Ministry of Education." The pattern has brought a tremendous blessing. We have flown about half the cabinet-level officials in the airplane and probably a dozen members of Parliament. They even know us by our first names.

I was out jogging one night, running along in my green shorts and tee shirt, when a car blinked its lights at me and pulled over. It was the Deputy Speaker of Parliament. "Edward," he called, "come over." I came over, panting, my hair hanging in my eyes, perspiration dripping off me. He said, "Have you seen Harold, the pilot?"

I said, "Harold is out on a flight, but I will see him tomorrow." He said, "I've got something for Harold." Then he reached in and brought out a bottle of honey, saying, "Harold flew me out to my town with medicine last week. I promised I would bring him some honey; this is it." The Deputy Speaker of Parliament was sending a gift to the pilot.

Ed Warnock
May 1979

Permission Is Not Enough

All of us who knew him agree that Uncle Cam Townsend was a man of tremendous vision. Not only did he have a vision of reaching people in their own language, but also of translating the Scriptures into their language so they would have the resources to carry on their own organization without outside help.

Although he was not the first Bible translator, I believe that, more than anyone else in this century, he saw the importance of small groups having the Scriptures in their own language. He also saw that missionaries were not needed permanently but should work themselves out of a job, and the quickest way was to provide the Scriptures. I'm sure we all agree he will be remembered for these basic emphases. But in some ways I feel his foresight in the methodology of what might be called "approach to governments " was just as important, and it is that topic I want to consider here.

Not only did he see the vision of Bible translation, he also saw and developed, as he led SIL, a completely new strategy with regard to learning and teaching by expatriates. In my view the latter is a separate contribution from the former and it is equally significant. His vision involved two breaks with the past. Perhaps this is why Wycliffe is so hard to understand.

It is hard to sum up this strategy in a single sentence but perhaps something like this would capture the idea: "Cooperate with the government rather than compete," as missions seem to do with their schools and medical work.

Evangelicals of his generation were suspicious of
foreign governments. In the U.S. they had been brought
up on the doctrine of the separation of church and state.
In addition, many held the view, at least subconsciously,
that politics and the political process were necessary
evils, generally "dirty" and something an evangelical
should avoid.

Uncle Cam went to the Scriptures for his instructions regarding a working strategy of cooperating with
governments. He found first of all that God is in charge
of the world. Romans 13:1, and following verses, teach
that the "powers that be are ordained by God." Therefore, we need to be subject to governments since they
have been established by God. And in verse seven we
find that we are to render to all their dues. This means we
render to the government the respect due it as a civil
power and cooperate with it in endeavors to do good for
its citizens. The holder of an office should be respected
because he holds that office (in spite of what his personal
moral life might be). He is God's instrument. We find in
Romans 9:17 that God raised up Pharaoh, who from our
vantage point could be called a brutal, barbaric
murderer. He enslaved the people of Israel and even
caused their children to be destroyed. Yet the Scriptures
say that God raised him up.

Therefore, host governments are God's instruments,
which we as expatriate Christians need to cooperate with,
to serve, to honor, instead of exposing or ignoring them.
In addition, we need to remember that we are guests of
the government of the country where we are located. The
government has legitimate control of the people in its
territory, so we should be cooperative and submissive.
Most governments have announced for their minority

peoples goals with which we can agree. Uncle Cam often pointed out to us that there is a great deal we can agree with and laud in governmental policy toward these minority groups, such as increased educational opportunities and improved medical facilities.

Uncle Cam also believed, as I understood him, that we must make whatever effort is necessary to maintain a close relationship with the government. This should be done in various ways:

1. We should call frequently on government officials and leave them some reminder of our program. (Linguistic reprints and literacy material are excellent items to leave.) We should call on officials regularly even though we may not have anything to ask for. We should report our activities to them. Uncle Cam reminded me of the importance of this once when we were making calls in Mexico. He said that if there had been questions or rumors about us, the officials would not have to locate us and call us in but would be able to talk to us on our next regular visit. This would save them and us the embarrassment of being called in to be interrogated over rumors that might be going around.

2. Uncle Cam believed we should have as many cooperative endeavors with governmental agencies as possible. Examples:

a. Our Centers and headquarters, where possible, should be on government land.

b. We should have general agreement with the government regarding the tribal locations where we work.

c. The bilingual school system in Peru is an illustration of a cooperative effort. This system is part of the official educational system, with the government appointing the director and paying the Indian school teachers. We provide the location for training at Yarina-cocha, and we cooperate in the preparation of Indian language material and the training of the teachers in their own languages. We help make the program go by supplying the necessary expertise, but it is an official program of the government and the government gets the credit for the operation. This is very much in line with Uncle Cam's feeling that service programs should be essentially government programs which we merely help.

d. The people-to-people program involving the "friendship fleet" of aircraft is another illustration of government involvement. A community in the U.S. provides an aircraft for the government of a country where we work with the understanding it will be for SIL use. At the time of the presentation of the plane, government officials participate in official ceremonies with SIL inconspicuously in the background. Title to the plane is held by the government, with the understanding that the plane is for our use. This means we are flying government planes.

e. In the early days in Tetelcingo, Uncle Cam would call on government officials and ask them for contributions of seed, trees or other help. This was to let the government officials know that as far as Uncle Cam was concerned, he wanted to be merely a part of the government's own program for helping Indians. He was perfectly willing to let them have the credit. He merely wanted the opportunity to serve, to quietly proclaim to the Indian people the love of Christ, and to translate the Scriptures.

It is extremely important to note at this point that in his view permission is not enough. Uncle Cam, if I understood him correctly, believed that simply getting the necessary permission from the government to do something would never satisfy the basic requirement of maintaining thing would never satisfy the basic requirement of maintaining a close relationship with the government in a program of mutual involvement. Nor does such a mutual program necessarily have to be always directly supportive of the minority groups. It can be a cooperative program whereby the citizens of the country are taught, or benefit by it. For example, Uncle Cam is not opposed to DC-3s or larger aircraft because they are large aircraft. Rather, he believes that any program involving DC-3s should somehow be a joint effort with either the government itself or an official airline of the government; thus we are providing additional training for pilots, or we are opening a new route for the official airline to take over at a later date, or something of the sort.

I repeat what I understand to be a very basic principle of Uncle Cam's thinking—that permission alone is not enough; there should be joint involvement between us and the government in as many programs as possible. Our posture then is service, cooperation, and a very close relationship with the government.

On the other hand, our profile in the country should be as low as possible, characterized by as much identification with people as possible, consistent with the kind of work which we need to do and the way it should be carried out. Several specific points come to mind which might illustrate this general principle.

1. Centers where we have fairly sizeable concentration of foreigners should be relatively isolated. As far as the general population is concerned, "out of sight, out of mind."

2. Houses and buildings on Centers should not be ostentatious. Airplanes should not be elaborately painted. Although these are relatively minor points, yet they are important. Too much paint on the outside can

tion. Uncle Cam felt that we should give an impression more along the line of what we really are: a moderately poor, somewhat struggling organization that is there to help and serve, one which puts its money into the service of the people rather than on external appearances. It is not that Uncle Cam was against efficiency and comfort.

I heard him say many times that he "likes the 'pie' in pioneering." He said, "Make your houses as comfortable as you like on the inside, but don't make a show of having them look too good on the outside."

3. We should not be too much in evidence in major cities but should be out in the villages doing the work. When we do have conferences and are in evidence in major cities, we should have as many government officials and national university people as possible visit.

Let me summarize the basic points made here. They are extremely important as far as our approach is concerned.

1. Don't be satisfied with permission; rather, involve the government with joint enterprises.

2. Avoid a high profile generally in the country. Identify closely with the people.

Ben Elson
INTERCOM 5.11,
November 1974

The Awful Airplane
and the
Bane of Branches

One of the signs of health in an organization is the ability to create new methods in the light of previous experiences or in new situations. I have been greatly encouraged by observing "signs of life" in the field of government relations. I have noted two developments in Africa that I think are worth sharing.

A good statement of the JAARS problem reads like this: "...SIL is the only entity with the ability to go and come easily, normally in airplanes, and communicate easily in backward areas of the country. This creates much jealousy and hurt pride in many sectors of the country."

Is such a criticism the inevitable result of employing technology to solve our logistics and communications problems? Or are creative alternatives possible that will turn our technological sophistication from a liability into an asset before host governments?

The Awful Airplane

Africa's Southern Sudan is a region starved for adequate transportation, in this respect not unlike many areas in which SIL works. A JAARS flight program was initiated to solve the transportation problem. Liability? Not so.

Under the direction of John Bendor-Samuel, the

Africa Area Director, the airplane serves under the name of the Ministry of Education (the agency with whom we have our agreement). The plane serves the Ministry of Education and SIL on an equal basis.

Every attempt is made to make the joint use of the aircraft a reality. The Ministry is consulted on major policy matters concerning the plane. They help us write our requests for operating permits, and most of the correspondence with Civil Aviation authorities is on Ministry of Education letterhead. The Director of the Ministry is encouraged to participate in the management of the flight program, and every opportunity for the government to use the plane on a cost-sharing basis is encouraged. Branch members are encouraged to refer to "the Ministry's airplane" when talking about the flight program.

The results have been pleasing. Many government officials have used the airplane. Some trips in the plane have been the occasion for friendships springing up between the SIL flight crew and government officials. Long evenings in distant towns have led to casual and effective interaction and hopefully to genuine friendships.

When other government agencies use the airplane, they must borrow it from the Ministry of Education, not from SIL. No attempt is made for SIL to hog the PR value of the plane. It is quite evident that the Minister of Education enjoys having access to his own air service and inviting other members of the government to fly with him.

This arrangement has helped many of the Regional Cabinet members and many members of the Regional Parliament to make flights to remote areas in the Ministry of Education/SIL plane. By being willing to lose some of the community relations value of the airplane, SIL has

SIL has also lost a good portion of the political liability of being a foreign organization operating an airplane in remote areas.

The strategy that was encouraged by the Africa Area Director has resulted in real progress in diffusing the "awful airplane" liability. The plane is viewed by many key elements in the government as the Minister of Education's plane. The Ministry of Education views the airplane as its own and supports its right to operate in remote and sensitive areas. SIL has had the opportunity to meet many key government officials and to demonstrate to the government that we are willing to commit our resources to help them find solutions to problems that we share.

Radio — the Bane of Branches

After the closing of an SIL branch in Africa, the director reported that the possession of radios by SIL teams contributed towards a situation that resulted in the non-renewal of our agreement. In another country the administration cancelled a planned center telephone system to avoid separating ourselves materially even further from our neighbors across the Center fence.

The question before us is not how to own radios and telephone systems and get away with it, but how we can communicate more rapidly and with greater reliability. A most remarkable thing happens when we restate the problem this way. The issue is no longer either national security or material wealth that separates us from the communities in which we live, but how to solve a problem we share with those communities. The key is to solve our problem in such a way that the community benefits, or else to help them solve their problem so that we enjoy the benefits of the improved situation.

In one African country an experiment is being tried.

SIL and the government experience identical communications problems with the Interior. In this situation SIL has offered to the local sponsoring agency our technical resources to help them solve *their* communications problems. Whatever solution is arrived at will be owned and operated by our sponsors. SIL will be a subscriber to their communications service.

The particular solution in this case was a network of two-way radios. SIL has loaned to the government agency one of our top JAARS radiomen. The government has made available an office in the Ministry of Education headquarters building, to be converted into a radio repair facility and communications center. The Ministry of Education has created staff slots for the radio technicians and radio operators on its payroll. The station licenses, including the ones for the SIL linguist teams in the field, will all be in the name of the Ministry of Education. The first SIL radio sits in the office of the Minister of Education, labelled "FIRST RADIO – MIN. OF ED. COMMUNICATIONS SYSTEM in cooperation with the Summer Institute of Linguistics."

Wherever possible, the radios will be located in government facilities – education offices, schools, or the home of the local headmaster. Some of the translators may have to walk across the village or town to get to the radio. It is anticipated, though, that this inconvenience will be more than compensated for by creating a mutually beneficial partnership with a key government agency. Our teams will have 75 percent of the benefit of a radio in their homes, but only a fraction of the political liability.

By helping the Ministry of Education solve their communications problems, a situation has been created where we in SIL do not need to have our own independent radio system. Reasonably adequate communications facilities are available to our teams through a government-owned-and-operated radio service.

If the situation arises in which the right of this radio system to function is questioned by powers within the country, there exists a key government agency which has a vested interest in the radios. SIL personnel should not need to become involved at all. This is as it should be. Local people will always know best how to deal with delicate issues that can have political, military or security overtones. Our credibility should be enhanced when local people of stature and responsibility represent our activities and projects to other government departments or agencies.

Ed Warnock
September 1978

We Would Appreciate Your Guidance

I have just read an article in a mission magazine telling how that mission has been invited into country X by SIL.

The mission is one which I love and believe in. Their people have been very good to us. You could even say that one of the reasons we are in country Y is because they (among others) invited us into that country.

But if we were to say that, it would give a misleading impression, just as their article gives a misleading impression of who has the authority to issue the invitation into country X.

Some countries, to be sure, authorize visas on the strength of invitations from national religious bodies in those countries to expatriate organizations. But the ultimate authority is not the inviting religious group but the government of the country in which that religious group operates. And the recognition of that authority should be explicit, not merely implicit.

In the early days of the work in Mexico, SIL had a wonderful relation with the Mexican Bible Society, especially with the national secretary, Hazael T. Marroquin, and his family. In fact, the SIL office was, for many years, in a room provided by the Bible Society. Cameron Townsend often consulted with Mr. Marroquin and received guidance from him.

But it was crystal clear to Mr. Marroquin, and especially to the President of the country, that Mr. Townsend looked first to the President of the country for guidance and only secondarily to Mr. Marroquin.

What about Peter's words, "We ought to obey God rather than man"? Following that principle, should not the counsel of Mr. Marroquin have outranked the guidance of the secular President of that country? Curiously, the people to whom Peter spoke those words were the religious leaders of their nation, not the secular government officials. He was rejecting the guidance of the religious hierarchy.

The divine alchemy, as Bill Gothard has so often pointed out, works in miraculous ways when we recognize the respective ranks of the authorities who are over us. Because Mr. Townsend recognized the rank and authority of the President as higher than that of Mr. Marroquin, the day came when, on the intercession of Mr. Townsend, a large shipment of Bibles which had been impounded by the government was ordered released to the Bible Society by the President. And the President further decreed that, from then on, Bibles should be allowed into the country duty-free.

RSP

The Senior Partners

Reporting as expatriates to national officials is basic. Even recognizing that civil officials outrank religious officials in the priority which should be given them is a part of the ABC's of SIL work overseas. Recognizing officials of the governments under which we work as senior partners in the work we do in those countries is a much higher order of responsibility.

When we wanted to start using aircraft and radios in the Philippines, for example, we were told that the use of airplanes would be permitted, but for foreigners to be allowed to use two-way radios in the Philippines would require an act of Congress. I knew therefore that we needed President Magsaysay as a senior partner in the effort.

When I took the matter up with the President, he said, "No problem. Give the Philippine Signal Corps title to the radios and they will authorize SIL to operate them."

But before the recommendation could be implemented, Magsaysay was killed in an airplane crash. Now what should we do?

We went to the Secretary of Defense and explained what the President had said. "Just consider that Magsaysay has never died," replied the secretary, making it plain that he would implement the recommendation. And he did.

We tried to make officials in India senior partners in

the work there and enjoyed good success on the state and local levels. In Maharashtra, Madya Pradesh and Andra Pradesh, local officials were cooperative and entered in a very friendly way into the work with us. Even in Delhi we were able to meet some of the highest officials, including Indira Gandhi. But we failed to establish anyone in residence in Delhi, with the result that, although many there were friendly to us, none of them looked on the SIL project as their own. As far as they were concerned, they were "outsiders looking in," rather than leading participants in the work we wanted to do.

Things went better in Nepal. Both the university and the federal government are based in Kathmandu, so it was a much simpler matter to relate to both at one and the same time. The vice chancellor of the university, for example, became the senior partner of the SIL work in that country in the finest sense of the word. So, when the project in that country was far enough along to make us feel the need of a linguistic center, he was consulted.

"I want the Center to be on the campus of the university," he replied, "so that the university may benefit from the contribution of your people." It was done as he requested. Not only the linguistic center but also an excellent printshop was established on the campus by SIL. Both the institute and the university profited from and enjoyed the patterns of cooperation which resulted.

The same was true of the JAARS program which was established in Nepal. Up to that time we had not heard of JAARS being required to carry a government observer on its flights in any country where it is at work. Because of the proximity to China, however, this was required in Nepal. "It is all right," the vice-chancellor assured us. "We will appoint various people from the university to accompany the plane on its flights. Both you and they will benefit."

And so it did indeed turn out. Members of the university staff were able to visit places which had previously been only names to them. And when questions were raised as to why Americans were flying small planes in Nepal, the university observer was the ideal person to verbalize for the pilot the reasons for the SIL presence in the country.

We were less successful in the linguistic partnership which we should have established. We did do a fine piece of work teaching and guiding Nepalis in linguistic analysis and writing. We even invested a substantial amount of money in helping give Nepalis linguistic training outside of Nepal. But at a crucial point we failed. Hardly any linguistic book or article appeared with the name of a Nepali as co-author.

This was tragic, and it need not have been. True, it is not often done by American scholars. But we did not need to regard the more common American academic traditions as sacrosanct. We had no less a man than Franz Boaz, father of American anthropology, as a model to show us that the person who provides most of the data for a given book or article has as much right to see his name on the title page as does the interpreter of the data. We missed many opportunities to dignify Nepalis by doing just that.

Fortunately things went differently in Indonesia. At our first major linguistic workshop in Irian Jaya there were Indonesians in attendance, writing papers as authors in their own right. And the final volume of collected papers, to Ken Pike's everlasting credit, appeared as edited by Ignatius Suharno and Kenneth Pike, in that order.

You can hardly imagine how good I felt, at the dedication of the first Helio-Courier airplane for service in Indonesia, to be able to present to the Ambassador of Indonesia, and to his cultural affairs officer, copies of this book, with Cenderawasih University on the title page as publisher and with an Indonesian faculty member from that university as first author. No wonder visas began to be issued to SIL applicants again not long after that occasion!

The Bilingual Schools Program

Perhaps the best illustration of the senior partner rank of government is the bilingual schools program in the countries where it is going on. When Mark and Esther Weathers were ready to offer to help on Tlapanec literacy, for example, Mark went to the Director of Education for that area with his material. The director liked it and had Mark talk with the supervisor. The supervisor asked Mark to explain the material to his 106 Tlapanec teachers. They were delighted. They and the government bought the whole program—orthography, readers and Spanish-via-Tlapanec procedure. It became the government's, organized and overseen by the director and supervisor, with Mark and Esther as consultants. It is *the* way to go.

RSP

Give Them a Piece
of the Action

Daws Trotman, in the early days of the Navigators, was so sold on the faith principle that when a person asked how he could help, Daws would reply, "The Lord takes care of us." Finally one of his friends took him aside and said, "Daws, you won't let your friends know how they can help you. That is not right."

Daws took the message to heart and changed his ways. From then on, he let his friends know how they could help. Years ago I asked Uncle Cam why he asked the Mexican government officials for help. He said, "The main resource a politician has is power. Power can be used either for you or against you. The best way to keep it from being used against you is to get it started going for you."

How often we have had occasion to see the truth of that point of view! Even after a man leaves office or dies, as in the case of President Magsaysay, bureaucratic precedent and inertia take over. When his successor has to make decisions, it is far easier to do so on the basis of precedent than to try to be original. If the precedent was to help you, the odds are high that you will be helped again.

The path of least resistance in government work is to expect an official to do only what is required of him in the line of duty. To expect and seek only this much, however, may mean that they and we will fall far short of God's best for both. Since it is their country, and since much of what we are doing is really their responsibility, the government officials should be offered as many opportunities as possible to help in ways which are beyond the call of duty. The following are some examples:

A high official in Indonesia's Ministry of Education offered rides in his car from Bogor to Jakarta. These were gratefully accepted.

A Mexican official was told of the need for eucalyptus trees in Tetelcingo. He was delighted to make a contribution of a large number of seedlings.

Officials and scholars from several different countries were asked to make enquiries regarding the well-being and whereabouts of John and Carolyn Miller while they were being held. There was very good response from many.

The Rector of Cenderawasih University invited Dick Pittman to be his house guest for several days; the invitation was gratefully accepted.

A former Bishop of Kontum was asked to help locate the former Minister of Education of Cambodia and notify him that his wife and children were alive and well.

A former Minister of the Interior of South Vietnam was asked to help on legal matters relative to SIL property use in South Vietnam and gladly did so.

Very many present and former officials of a large number of countries have gladly given notes and letters of introduction when asked to do so.

Aaron Saenz, a distinguished Mexican leader, made several large contributions to the building of the SIL Center in Tlalpan, Mexico.

Engineer Cuauhtemoc Cardenas, son of the late President Lazaro Cardenas, contributed architectural work in the planning and building at SIL Tlalpan.

Mrs. Magsaysay wrote an introduction to the biography of Gaspar Makil.

Rafael Ramirez, after questioning the use of Indian languages, contributed $5.00 to the Townsends' garden in Tetelcingo. It did much to change his outlook. Distinguished citizens of many countries have gladly given time to serve on advisory councils in their respective countries.

When the Townsends were injured in a commercial plane crash in Chiapas, former President Cardenas marshalled all available help for them, including even the state governor, in the plane which went to their aid.

Numerous officials, including several presidents and ambassadors, have participated in good-will airplane ceremonies at home and abroad.

The total effect of these gestures has been to make them feel that the SIL work is *their* work, not a program of outsiders competing against them.

Of course, there are boobytraps. One of the worst is to give the impression that it is a foreign project which is being helped, rather than a project of the host country which is being helped by the foreigner. In order to keep that misunderstanding from developing, it is important for expatriates, when they use first person plural pronouns (we, us, our, ours) in communications to national officials, to make sure these are understood as first person inclusive rather than exclusive. That is, the meaning must be perceived as "the project for which you and we are responsible" rather than "the project which we (foreigners) are running without your participation."

Even the naming of a project can make or break it. In Indonesia, for example, we talked a few times about the "Summer Institute of Linguistics Cenderawasih University" project before we realized that it had to be "Cenderawasih University-Summer Institute of Linguistics" project.

I've Got a Great Idea.

In this connection, it is amazing to see how much good can be done if a person does not care who gets the glory for it. It was election time in a great South American republic. The candidates were out for votes. Obviously, to get them, they had to have inspiring platforms. And they did. Nearly all included in their plans a bilingual education plank. They would teach Indian children to read first in their own mother tongue. Then they would use this skill as a basis for teaching Spanish. It was a popular idea – sure to win votes.

No one explained that the idea had reached the country through a gringo. And the gringo, Uncle Cam, was the last one to want them to explain. He was delighted that each aspirant put it forward as his own idea. That was a crucial part of its success.

I cannot recall how I came to realize that most missions (and missionaries) regard themselves as competitors with the governments of the countries in which they work. But it is surely true. Very few are prepared to allow the governments to be partners in the work they are doing. Still fewer are willing for the governments to get the glory for what they do. And only an infinitesimal number know how to ghost-write the script for inspired government programs and remain anonymous afterward.

Uncle Cam is certainly one of the minuscule group. And one of his secrets is obviously his refusal to let past failures and discouragements cloud his vision or dull his enthusiasm. Another is his consummate care to make sure that officials of the host government get the glory for any noteworthy achievements, and especially for having generated the idea in the first place.

Some object that if we look for guidance to government officials who are not of the same religious persuasion as we, we will be led in ways we do not want to go. But God has marvelously used such men on innumerable occasions to lead in ways which are clearly God's ways. Jim Dean, for example, often said to the Director of Deccan College in India, "We would appreciate your guidance." And he was never disappointed.

Not the least of our eminently satisfying activities in India was our relationship with that Director. We continually sought his advice, and he, with equal faithfulness, gave it.

Nor was his guidance in error. He told us to whom to relate in Delhi, and how. He introduced us personally. He gave us a letter to the head of another large institution on the other side of India, who in turn introduced us to the Collector of a large district in which we wanted to work. This man in turn enabled us to start.

Would it not have been better to ask the missions to guide us? No. However successful the missions might have been, God has made the government officials, not the missionaries, the stewards over the land and people in which they live. We who seek to live and work there are dependent on the officials both for permission and for direction.

True, they sometimes sent us to the missionaries for advice. That is the way it worked in Irian Jaya. It is vital, however, to remember that we went to the officials first, and from them to the missionaries, with official blessing. It is also important to remember that we went not only to the Protestants but also to the Catholics. It is the way the government guided.

One day the most influential of the Catholic Fathers drove up to our door with a rare, out-of-print book in his hand. "This book is not supposed to leave our library," he said, "but I know the government has asked you to study the languages of the Valley of the Tor. And reference materials about them are scarce. So we want to loan you this book, *The People of the Tor.*"

It was the book we needed most!

RSP

The Patronato Pattern

Friends of SIL

There is a profound sense in which we get wrong answers because we ask wrong questions, or because we ignore crucial answers which have been given but not listened to. At a time when the expression "national involvement" is on many lips, almost no one is heard talking of national sponsoring committees of statesmen whose stature commands national and international respect. There is no great problem in generating enthusiasm among young idealists for Bible translation work. Even the organization of committees of evangelicals to sponsor national translators is not overly difficult. But the formation of "Friends of SIL" committees of distinguished national leaders is something else. There are several true success stories in which this has been accomplished, however.

But why should there be such committees? Is it not enough to form groups like the Translation Committee of the Philippines and pass the vision of Bible translation on to them? The answer is No. And the reason is simple. Since the days when Israel rejected theocratic rule, God has given top authority and responsibility, worldwide, to civil rather than religious governments. And it is now the civic leaders, rather than the religious ones, who make the decisions which most fundamentally "bind" or "loose" Bible translators to do their work in each country where it is needed. The following description of a meeting of the Mexican Patronato may help illustrate.

The Installation of Amalia Cardenas

What good is an advisory committee? It is largely an honorary (i.e., no work expected) group; it is hard to find meaningful matters on which to ask their advice, and it is embarrassing to know what to do if they give advice which is difficult to follow.

In July 1976 I was invited by the Mexican Branch to spend a week in Mexico helping with arrangements for a ceremony at which the widow of former President Lazaro Cardenas was to be installed as President of the Patronato (advisory or sponsoring committee) for SIL-Mexico. I accepted, and was involved in several of the activities preceding the installation, as well as the main ceremony itself.

One of the principal preparatory activities was inviting the guests. I was paired with Jose Estrella, and we were asked to invite the Ambassadors of India, Indonesia, Vietnam, the Philippines, Peru and Colombia.

It may seem presumptuous for SILers to be calling on Ambassadors, but none of them could be insulted by being invited to a dinner at which the guest of honor was a person so distinguished as Mrs. Cardenas. As it turned out, because Mrs. Cardenas had accepted the invitation only a short while before it was necessary to hold the dinner, none of the Ambassadors I invited were able to attend. But Jose and I were given hour-long interviews with the Ambassadors of India and Indonesia in which both of them expressed considerable interest in the work of SIL. We were not able to see any ranking official in the Vietnamese embassy, but good ground work was laid for the time when it will be possible to meet some higher person there. The invitation to the Ambassador of the Philippines surely did us good.

The Ambassador of Colombia could not come, but

Uncle Cam was able to be with us in a surprisingly long conversation with the number two man, and to strengthen very much the SIL position in Colombia through that conversation.

Serious attempts were made to invite the President of Mexico and the Minister of Education to the function. Neither could come, but both named the head of the National Indian Institute – an outstanding scholar and old friend – to represent them. He made an eloquent speech at the dinner, which did SIL great good.

I had the privilege of sitting beside the number two man of the Indonesian Embassy at the dinner; I am sure it was very meaningful to him.

The widow of a former Minister of Education (Jaime Torres Bodet) who had been President of the Patronato, the widow of a former Minister of Finance (Ramon Beteta) who had been a close friend of Mr. Townsend, and the widow of a former Mexican Ambassador to Peru (Moises Saenz) were present, adding lustre to the occasion. President Cardenas' son, Engineer Cuauhtemoc Cardenas, stood beside his mother during the ceremony. Other members of the Patronato were present, as well as many distinguished scholars, officials, and old friends. The total impact for SIL was incalculable.

Xerxes, Artaxerxes, and Cyrus

The point is this: Just as God gave us the priceless birthright of two organizations – WBT and SIL – so He has given us another incomparable birthright – the Mexican SIL Patronato pattern. If we despise, trade it off, or give it away, as Esau did his, we will have no one but ourselves to blame for the tragic results.

If, on the other hand, we embrace it and capitalize

on it, marvelous fruit, lasting throughout eternity, will result.

It is important to clarify that the function of a patronato, while it may be largely honorary, should not be exclusively so. Busy and distinguished nationals cannot be kept interested for long unless they too are given activities worthy of their stature.

Some SIL members are hesitant to ask outstanding nationals who are not declared evangelical Christians to help in SIL work. Many such nationals, however, are longing for ways to help enterprises like SIL because they sense the benefit which will result for their country.

Xerxes, Artaxerxes, Darius the Mede, and Cyrus helped when asked. Why not follow the precedent of those who sought their help?

RSP

II

Love in Shoe Leather

One Doctor of Philosophy told us:
"I feel like this is a different planet.
I have never seen such unity and love.
I do not know what you have,
but it is really different."
We told him it was the Lord.

— Millie Lyon

I Put Myself
in His Shoes

"As I sat in the office of the people responsible for the affairs of indigenous peoples, I began to see that in the past whenever I came in with an idea, problem or question, the amount of interest that I received from them was directly related to whether or not what I had to offer, or the problem I had to solve, was helping them solve a problem they were facing. If it created a new problem, their help was generally nil; however, if it was helping them solve a serious problem they were having, and (this is important) my idea was of very little risk to their personal positions in the department, then I got a lot of help.

"With this in mind, I began to make a list of pressures my friend was under. Later I told him that I had made this list and really felt for him. As I read the list, his reddening eyes told me that no one had ever cared enough to show that much interest in the load the man was carrying. The following is the list I read off to him:

1. International pressure — Countries criticize them.

2. Religious pressure — Some religious leaders are always after them.

3. Security pressure — The government is always checking security.

4. Scientific pressure — Scientists want to study tribal groups.

5. Tribal pressure — Tribal people want promises fulfilled.

6. Landlord pressure — They want land problems resolved.

7. Bureaucratic pressure — They want higher wages.

8. Economic pressure — Developers want resources from tribal lands.

9. Health pressure — Tribal people need health care.

10. Educational pressure — Tribal people need educational help.

11. Transportation pressure — It's hard to get to the tribal locations.

12. Financial pressure — There is more work than there is money.

13. Family pressure — All of the above affect their relations with their families.

"After I had made the list it was easier for me to plug into my friend's problems. After going over the list with him I asked if we could help them with transportation. The answer was a definite Yes."

(Name omitted by request)

A Government Relations
Flight to the Jungle

Dear Uncle Cam,

We thank you most sincerely for the $100 gift given for government relations. We used it to help pay for a PR flight carrying some officials and TV folks from La Paz to Tumi Chucua. The total cost was somewhat over $1,200.

The people who came from La Paz and Cochabamba were not the ones we originally hoped would come. There was no minister or undersecretary, but the National Director for Rural Education, who has been very opposed to bilingual education, was able to come. He had been exposed to some "radical" aspects of bilingual education in which books were published without Spanish. This turned him off. When he saw our primers with both the Indian language and Spanish, he thought that approach was a good compromise and was willing to accept it. He appears to have been convinced of some of the value of the bilingual education after seeing the demonstration and the courses in session. On my next visit to La Paz he was extremely cordial and expressed again his appreciation for our having shown him the program, rather than just telling him about it.

Another person who came was a professor from a university in Santiago, Chile. He is a very distinguished, highly educated gentleman, who speaks approximately 15 languages, with special studies in Mapuche and Quechua. He is a very avid reader of the Bible. After visiting Tumi Chucua and being duly impressed, he was giving a series of lectures in one of the far-left universities. On the final evening of his lectures, he became very emotional as he expressed what the Institute was doing at Tumi Chucua through bilingual education. He centered most of his talk on this subject. The student body gave him a standing ovation, did not want him to leave, continued to ask him many questions, and sometime later accompanied him to his hotel to talk more about bilingual education and the impact it has on the development of the Indians.

Our procedure for the visitors after their arrival was first a welcoming speech given in the hangar with coffee and tea and then a display of some of the handwork of the indigenous women. The group was divided into five sections. Perry Priest, Associate Director Field Operations; Don Van Wynen, Director of Leadership Training Course; Terry Smith, who was also active in the course and works in Community Development; John Ottaviano, a linguist; and I led the company on a guided tour of our Center, covering the various aspects of our work. In the 1-1/2 hour period they saw our Tumi Chucua facilities and ten different classes in session. Following this, we had lunch and then a short program in the dining room. This was followed by a fantastic downpour of rain which kept us all indoors a while before we departed again for La Paz. That night we were given a 3-minute coverage on the national TV which was seen in all of the major cities of the country. It was a very favorable report. We have also had some articles in the newspaper as a result of this and other visits of press personnel to Tumi Chucua.

It is expensive to come to Tumi Chucua, but I believe it has been worth the effort both in time and money. We feel it must be done if we are going to impress the government with the reality of what we are doing; we must be able to request from them things that Bolivia's ethnic peoples are going to need and which SIL cannot provide once our work is finished.

Your brother,
Dave Farah

A Different Planet

Letter to Uncle Cam from Floyd and Millie Lyon
of Peru, whose son, Nathan, was killed in the crash
of a commercial plane there.

Yarinacocha
May 17, 1978

Dear Uncle Cam and Elaine:

So many exciting things are happening in Peru that we have been wanting to share them with you. It has been tremendous to see how the Lord continues to direct, and to give opportunities to share His Word, not only with the Indians, but with the local business people and with officials in high places.

You may know that since last July Floyd has been full time in public relations, but maybe you do not know how a pilot got into that position. Let me fill you in on a bit of history.

When we first came to Peru 20 years ago, we had an excellent Spanish course in Lima, lived with a Peruvian family, and therefore had a good foundation for living in the culture. After our months in Ecuador we began at Yarinacocha but fell into the social/cultural trap that Vi Escobar had warned us about. The base was big, I was busy with my babies, and Floyd was away flying a lot, so it was easy to entertain here on the base and not really become involved with those around us. That big invisible wall around the base kept us in. There were some exceptions, such as working in Spanish literacy with you, Elaine, and some trips to local villages, but we were not really getting involved in depth.

Then came the revolution about 10 years ago, when U.S.-Peru relations were so strained. It looked quite possible that we might have to leave the country. What struck Floyd and me was that if we left then, there would not be a single Peruvian who would really care. Perhaps a few carpenters to whom we gave work, or our maid, but not really close friends. We promised the Lord then that if He should choose to allow us to remain, we would do everything possible to have an outreach to the Peruvians.

Hospitality

We stayed and began seeking the Lord's direction. I wrote to Evie Elder, Nadine Burns, Gloria Wroughton and Doris Anderson, asking for pointers on entertaining Peruvians in our home. After about 8 years the book that began with that collection of information was finally printed and we use it today — *Peruvian Culture*. Doris had to teach me how to properly greet Peruvian women! The Riches were also a big help. We began inviting local officials into our home, one or two couples at a time, so we could really get to know them. My first try was to invite the wife of the Mayor of Puerto Callao to our home for a tea. A number of our women came. This wife (French-Canadian married to a Peruvian) was not very outgoing, and the only thanks I ever had from her came from a secondhand source. Her comment was that our women spoke Spanish badly! So began my try at Peruvian entertaining.

There were some questionable times when officials of one office accepted and then did not show up. That was during a crisis. The Velies had joined us in inviting them for supper. We did some praying about that, for we did not know what had happened. It turned out to be just car trouble and they came at a later date, but we had a good prayer meeting over it anyway! Then there was the head of the army, a Lt. Colonel who was quite a joker, but we did not know it. He marched in with his wife, looked our house over and said, "It's better than where I live! I'm going to move in!"

Plane to Desk to People

But those were all learning times. Floyd flew for 12 years, then had the flight coordinator job. He never officially terminated flying, but it began to be evident that he could not actively fly and run the office. So for seven years he "flew" a desk. He does not miss flying, but does miss the contact with the tribes. During those years I was working in PR, especially with the annual bilingual education closing ceremony (clausura). So Floyd and I did lots of entertaining still. But when you realize that Peruvian hours can easily lead to midnight, or to 1 or 2 a.m., and that a flight coodinator's radio contacts began at 7:30 a.m., you can see what a drain this was on Floyd. And running the flight office is a very difficult job, because as the in-between man trying to do what is best for both the linguists and the tribes, there are so many factors which he cannot control.

When Jerry Elder came through here a year ago April, we talked with him, because we knew physically we could not continue. It was by his suggestion that Floyd went full-time into PR. I still had the responsibility of writing daily bulletins, a job which I had been doing for the past eight years. I feel the Lord has been in this, but about a month ago I felt I should stop. Ruth Cowan is currently doing a fine job, but as she is also director's secretary, this puts a load on her. She writes in Spanish for the radio, and then in both Spanish and English for the bulletin board and Lima House.

We do everything we can here in the Peru Branch to try to keep the gang together. We have been through many trials. But praise God, although there are times we disagree (as in any family), there is such a spirit of unity here that we are always glad to return to Peru after furloughs.

I failed to mention also that 10 years ago Floyd was invited to join the Rotary Club. We are the only gringos in it, although from time to time we have taken visitors from ILV. It is not easy to be members because of the hours, the expense, etc., but it has been one of the most satisfying experiences in real friendships that we have had. We have lots of plans for getting more of our folks involved when we return.

But back to what I started with...The most exciting thing to us has been these groups from Lima. They come out as names on a list, with titles, and within a day or so are friends, calling us by first names and using the "tu" form! And what they feel at our Center makes all the late hours worthwhile.

As time drew near for the clausura, having talked with R. last year, and having been in agreement with her that our members did not get involved enough, we had written up these suggestions and a schedule for this year's clausura. This was what we went by. Our members cooperated beautifully and had guests in many homes two by two. So friendships were begun. The bilingual teachers were involved in the meals and other activities, and the Lord blessed. We incorporated music in the banquet program this year and feel the Lord used that to create (or help create) a good atmosphere. I am sure you have heard favorable reports from the Minister of Education and others.

One Doctor of Philosophy told us, "I feel like this is a different planet. I have never seen such unity and love. I do not know what you have, but it is really different." We told him it was the Lord. He did not agree, but he kept saying, "You are really different."

Another clausura guest was a historian and teacher at the Catholic University who had brought his wife and eight- and nine-year-old children. When we gave the wife a copy of the Psalms in Spanish, she thanked us profusely and said, "We did not bring our children with us to see the jungle; we wanted them to know you all, to see how you live and to know God."

To Our Party

We have had clausura-like times ever since Christmas. January 30 we gave ourselves an anniversary party. Since being with our Rotary friends at so many functions, we could see their desires to have a good time, but it is always the same: some drinking and dancing with terrifically loud music. The women love to come to my birthday tea each September. This year I planned to skip it because I was recovering from surgery; before I could say so, they told me they were coming out but not to do anything fancy! The year when it looked as if we were leaving, we dropped out of Rotary for a few weeks; but about a month after my birthday, when we went to a dinner, three different ladies told me, "We missed your birthday, but we want to come out. When can we come?" So we had a birthday a month late and they came laden with gifts.

We had missed having a traditional 25th anniversary celebration, so we chose our 30th to invite our Peruvian friends. We invited our members also and had about 150

in the dining room. It was a rainy night, and many of the
Peruvians ended up walking to get here. But the Lord really put that evening together. It was nothing that we did
at all. There were several musical numbers, Lambert
spoke briefly, the Rotary president spoke, and then we
were touched when Prof. Tapia asked to make a speech.
Padre Clemente prayed, and we found out later that he
wanted to speak. Floyd made up slides of our life and
they ended with photos of Peru, with Debbie Hudson
singing "Mi Peru." We are still hearing comments about
that evening from our Rotary friends, Pucallpa officials
and others.

Elaine and Uncle Cam, I trust you take this letter in
the spirit in which it is written. I do not mean to build us
up; that is not my point at all. I just want to share with you
what the Lord is doing, how He is touching lives, and allowing us to be a little part of it. That anniversary celebration showed us what He can do, and how hungry these
people are for a "sane" fiesta, as that evening was called
by some of them. The fact that we did not serve any kind
of alcoholic drinks really struck them. And the Peruvians
love music. We have plans for doing more of this kind of
thing for the local folks, not just the Lima guests. Floyd
has many opportunities on a one-to-one basis with these
men. He had hoped to start a Bible study in Pucallpa, but
the sheer load of duties, plus the fact that we are still getting our priorities squared away in this job, and that we
also need some rest, has delayed him from doing it.

One other item on this anniversary really humbled
and touched me. I have had some interchange with the
Lions Club ladies, but do not really know more than two
or three of them. About a month ago one of the ladies
called me and said, "Because many of our ladies were in
Lima and others could not come because of the rain, we
missed your anniversary celebration. We want to give you

a tea. When can you come?" So that week I was honored by 15 ladies (and only knew three by name at the beginning) with a tea at the Mercedes, and given a lovely bracelet with pearls. The one lady who had attended described the celebration; they made speeches, and then I did. (One priority on furlough is to better our Spanish! Floyd is way ahead of me, though.) So I have another wide-open door to reach out to this group of ladies. I took one woman home that evening and discovered that her son has also died in the LANSA crash. These are the opportunities we do want to follow up.

Getting It All Together

When Dr. B., who is running for President, came to the jungle, he asked R.C. if he could visit Yarina. He wanted to have breakfast and a tour of the Center. Although we do not mix in politics, Lambert did not feel that we could turn him down. The Saturday night they were in Pucallpa it rained hard and the roads were in terrible shape. Lam was in town with us for dinner and he tried to suggest cancelling the breakfast since they could have problems getting to their next engagement. B. said, "If it takes all day, we are going to visit ILV. These people have got to see the work"...so they came! We had the breakfast at our home instead of at the dining room, feeling it was better for atmosphere to have it in a home; also there would be less distracting group activity. We had about 40 for breakfast and a delightful time. I had talked with Mrs. B. the day before. She lost a daughter on the first LANSA crash at Cuzco so we had much to share. She is a lovely Christian. The group was here about two hours, and our sons stayed with us.

The Minister of Education was so impressed by the bilingual teachers and their needs that he became determined to centralize bilingual education and get it in the hands of the Indians. To this end he sent out a commission of top-level education people to work out the details. I think this will be the basis for our contract, or have a lot to do with it.

In the meantime, we had been denounced again and were once again to be investigated on the old charges. But as always God is still running things, and the General in charge of the investigation is an old friend. He timed his coming to coincide with the close of the other commission, so they could report their findings.

That week was like running a six-ring circus, except that it was much more serious. Lambert needed to get to board meetings and we had these two commissions which overlapped two days instead of six hours, plus looking after the needs of all three members of the committee, a mother of one of the officials, a wife of a General and R. unexpectedly...and everyone had a different schedule! But it was one of the most exciting weeks we have ever had.

I just want to share three things about it. Weather had delayed a flight to the communities and I asked the General if he had seen the communications center. He had not, so we walked over together. As we crossed the airstrip, the General said to me, "Who would have thought six years ago that God would put me in this position to be of help to all of you!" We looked at the plaque on the door, and then inside at Nathan's photo, and talked with the Peruvian operator. The General had known Nathan personally and we had spent some time with him right after the memorial services following the crash in which Nathan was killed. He said, "The others have to see this." (They had seen our anniversary slides which include Nathan.)

The three men came over (a General and two

Colonels) and the General told them, "The Lord directs our lives just as He chooses. On the LANSA airplane he placed the passengers. Harold Davis had tried for days to find a plane to get home to his family for Christmas. The co-pilot had a flat tire on the way to the airport and was replaced at the last minute. One of the stewardesses that I had flown with just a few days before had switched routes with another and was aboard this plane." I explained about Nathan's having two reservations by mistake and having chosen the 24th to give him extra time to Christmas shop for the family; because of this one of our linguists, Pete Landerman, is alive today. He took Nathan's reservation for the 23rd instead of using his own on the 24th. The General said, "One of my best friends was going on the plane, could not get some urgent business papers (which were later found right in the office) and had to cancel. I too had a reservation on the LANSA plane, but the day before the flight my daughter begged me to stay home for Christmas, so I also cancelled." As I relived the LANSA story again with those men, my thought was, "Praise the Lord! Although they are dead, yet they are still being used by Him." The three listeners were touched; only the Lord knows how this witness of the Christian General will be used in their lives.

At breakfast the day they returned to Lima, we were sitting around our table, thirteen of us. Jim Wroughton gave a Psalm to the General and asked him to read. After he read there was quite a discussion of the Word. At least one, perhaps two or three of the guests, were unsympathetic with our work. It was a moving experience.

At the airport each member of the four-man investigation commission individually thanked Floyd and me, expressing admiration for what he had seen. One Colonel said, "I feel that I have been on a spiritual retreat. I feel clean. My wife will not know what happened to me."

So that is a bit of what Floyd and I have been engaged in. This is just one small part of the work as support personnel, so the linguists can continue translation. John Tuggy and Lorrie Anderson finish up with three Candoshis this week on the final revision of the New Testament. The Capanahua New Testament is 1/3 through...camera-ready copy will be filmed and taken to Dallas in July, or somewhere for printing. Olive Shell has finished, and others are getting there. There is a new pilot program with the several dialects of Campa in which seven teams are working together to finish the job by 1985 or sooner.

The Colombian Ambassador and his wife are friends. The wife of the U.S. Ambassador and a party of six were here last week. We love these dear Peruvian friends and long to see them know our Saviour. Some do, and we do praise Him for that.

Love and prayers,
(signed) Floyd and Millie Lyon

The Fantastic
"Love...Bless...Do Good"
Theory

"I grew up three miles from the nearest Roman Catholic church. I did not know any Catholic in my home town as a friend. My custom as I grew up was to avoid Catholics and, in some Pharisaical manner, pray for them. Then I attended orientation lectures for prospective members of SIL and heard the fantastic idea of applying Matthew 5:43-48 in relationships with Roman Catholics. I liked the idea, but it was still theory."

With that introduction, Marjorie Croft proceeds to tell, in a chapter entitled, "Behold How Good and How Pleasant," of the transformation which took place in her during the course of the translation of the Munduruku New Testament in Brazil.

But it was not just in relations with Roman Catholics that the transformation took place. The often maligned National Indian Foundation came to the rescue of the Munduruku people in a notable way during a bad measles epidemic. Marge and her partner, Margaret Sheffler, worked shoulder to shoulder with them in a heroic effort which, under God's good hand, saved every life but one in a group which has no natural immunity to measles and which might easily have suffered many fatalities.

Two distinguished Brazilian scholars, who could have been snubbed through suspicion or ignorance, proved to be exceedingly helpful when their help was sought and thankfully accepted.

People who have lived most of their lives among civilians may mistrust or shun the military. In the very isolated habitat of the Munduruku, however, the Brazilian Air Force proved to be an indispensable lifeline. Not just once but many times their efficient, courteous help proved priceless not only to the translators but also to the Munduruku themselves.

Mid-Mission Baptists, New Tribes Mission, and Swiss Baptists could conceivably have been regarded as competitors or rivals. By throwing the girls several times on the mercy of these other groups, however, the Lord built a lovely tapestry of interdependence between them which bore fine fruit. And the staff of the Roman Catholic St. Francis Mission showed such love and faithfulness in helping Marge and Ilse Braun Bearth that their names must loom large in the list of those who helped bring the Munduruku New Testament into existence.

As Marge and her partners translated the fantastic "love...bless...do good" theory into both words and practice, both they and the Munduruku were metamorphosed into the image of God which, at creation, had been intended for them.

RSP

I Have "HER" on Board

I have sat in meetings where Uncle Cam reminded us to love our "enemies," to be kind to them, and to serve them. God gave me a personal experience of this in March 1979.

Some three years earlier the bilingual school system in Peru was decentralized from the Ministry of Education, and administration was put in the hands of the "nucleos" (regional schools) which are right out where the bilingual teachers are. This was good in some areas, but caused difficulties in others. In one place the local administrators even burned some of the books that were published for the bilingual school system. In one area, San Lorenzo on the lower Maranon, there was a former nun who was given authority to direct this program out in the jungle. Some of the bilingual teachers were fired; others were harassed. I guess we tend to consider such administrators our "enemies." But Leo Lance urged us to pray for this person rather than hate her.

One day in March I had a trip out to Barranca, with supplies for Peruvian young people working alongside SIL. As I prepared to leave, the commandante asked if I would take one of his teachers in. I said, "Sure, I'm going back empty, and I would be happy to take your teacher in." I put her and her baggage in the plane.

As I was making the last check, making sure everything was ready for take-off, a missionary met me at the far wing. He said, "Do you know whom you have on board?"

I said, "No, I don't."

He said, "That's the one who has been giving all these problems to the bilingual school effort."

I did not know what to say—she was in the airplane and all ready to go. So I said, "Great. Let's go."

I took off and God impressed me that I should get in touch with the Center. I did not know how to do that discreetly. Our aircraft frequency is routinely monitored, so I decided to try to get hold of Leo, who was our chief pilot and who was also flying. I turned to VHF and said, "I've got X on board. What shall I do?"

He said, "Call the director." I changed to the tribe frequency and called Eugene Loos. All he said when he found out who I had on board was, "I'll see you at the airplane." I was going a little faster than anticipated—had a tailwind—so I slowed the airplane a bit, got the gear down, and made sure that Eugene would be there when I arrived.

Sure enough, when I landed he was there. I taxied up to the pad and shut down. By the time I got out he had already opened the door and introduced himself to the passenger. He got her bag and they were standing beside the wing when I walked up. She turned to me and said, "How much do I owe you?"

I referred her to Eugene, who replied, "This is by courtesy of the Institute." Then he offered her a ride in a vehicle that was going into Pucallpa and put our Center services at her orders—whatever she needed.

Because of the way she had been treating us and the bilingual school system, she felt embarrassed. She tried to grab her bag out of Eugene's hand and head for the lake to hire transport. But Eugene kept the bag and went with her to the lake edge. The Lord saw to it that no commercial transport came, so they stood there, making conversation. Leo went in and got a coke for her. The last I saw my passenger, she was going up the hill on the back of Eugene's motor scooter.

The next Sunday Eugene spoke in our morning service and told the rest of the story. He chauffeured her as his guest around the facilities on the Center. When she finally started for Pucallpa in the vehicle that she had been offered by Eugene, she turned to him and said how overwhelmed she was at the kindness she had received on the flight and during her short time there.

It was a real joy to be a part of this experience.

Fred McKennon
Peru

On Pollution and Purity

It was only a pig, caught in the mud under a rail fence. The man passing by was not its owner but a person who was to become one of his country's most distinguished Presidents. Disregarding the mud which would be splattered on his good clothes, Abraham Lincoln unhesitatingly turned aside and freed the pig from the predicament into which it had fallen.

I was raised in a germ-conscious generation. Breathing the air of one with a cold could give me a cold. Kissing the lips of one with a cough could give me a cough. Drinking from the same glass someone else had used could give me who knows what!

What is wrong with that? Don't doctors and nurses use antiseptic procedures in hospitals? Did not Pasteur himself show how important it is to pasteurize milk and sterilize utensils? How much we owe to those who practice his principles of purity!

The achievement and maintenance of purity is commonly sought by two means: 1. avoidance of pollution; 2. attack on the pollution in such a way as to neutralize or overcome it.

It was during a typhoon in Manila that my appendix burst. I did not know it at the time, but when I was finally gotten to the operating table, a good many hours had elapsed and peritonitis had set in. How thankful I am that the nurses and surgeons did not elect to handle my septic condition by avoidance! True, they wore rubber gloves, masks over nose and mouth, and used carefully sterilized equipment. But armed with those resources and with proven ruptured appendix procedures, they pulled me safely out of a condition which could have been fatal.

Jesus was not wearing rubber gloves and a mask when He consorted with publicans and sinners. Nor did He boil His cutlery when He ate with Pharisees. But He was not avoiding the contamination which could have come from that close contact. He was treating it — with truth and compassion, Scripture and service.

Not everyone is qualified to do this, just as not everyone is qualified to perform appendectomies. But thank God for those who are!

RSP

We Can Help Win
Friends for Your Country

The scene was a familiar one: A foreigner sitting in front of a desk, expounding the value of linguistics, literacy and translation, an official sitting behind the desk shaking his head No. The foreign proposal, according to the official, was "exactly wrong" for his country.

"But we could help win friends for your country," averred the foreigner.

The official's reply is not known. But the foreigner's batting average, performing on his promise, is impressive. For example:

1. At a time when few had anything good to say about Mexican education, Cameron Townsend wrote a complimentary article on the subject which won the appreciation of the President of Mexico and the American Ambassador to Mexico.

2. When Mexico expropriated the properties of the foreign oil companies which refused to accept the Mexican Supreme Court's findings, Townsend not only wrote a pamphlet in defense of the Mexican position, but also sent copies of it to the legislators in Washington and went personally to Washington and New York to explain the Mexican position to legislators and oil company officials.

3. Townsend's biography of Cardenas, with editions both in Spanish and English, won enormous good will for Mexico all over the world. "It is the book," explained a Filipino aide, "which lit a fire in the soul of Magsaysay."

4. Though many countries of Asia are adamantly opposed to bilingual education as they understand it, Townsend's book, *They Found a Common Language*, not only makes a persuasive case for the principle, but also has won new respect all over the world for Mexico, Peru and the USSR. I saw personally the light of understanding dawn on the face of a brilliant Chinese educator in Laos years ago as I expounded the points made in the book.

5. For the people of the USA, who have been almost solidly opposed to the USSR since World War I, the Townsends published a book, *The USSR As We Saw It*, which has done much to convince people of good will, both in the USA and the USSR, that one couple at least practice Christ's command to "love your neighbor as yourself." The colorful ethnocentric amusement expressed by western writers describing other cultures one and two hundred years ago has now been replaced by caustic politicocentric ridicule of all who differ with our form of government. But Christ had those "different ones" in mind when He said, "Love your enemies, bless those who curse you, do good to those who hate you, pray for those who persecute you." One way to do it is by writing about them information which is admirable.

RSP

The SECAG Is Coming

The other day we saw an excellent example of Wycliffe teamwork. Ben Needham and I had gone to a nearby college to pay our respects to the Secretary of Agriculture. On the way back to Nasuli, we found that the Secretary had stopped at one of the villages by the road-side to greet some of the people. We stopped and invited him to visit our Center, thinking that surely he would not have time to do so. He said that he would be glad to stop by and would be there in a few minutes.

Uncle Ben and I rushed on ahead in the car to give as much advance notice as possible to our members. I left Uncle Ben at the gate to show the Secretary and his party where to drive in, then drove to each of our Center cottages in Paul Revere fashion, informing folk that the Secretary of Agriculture would be on the Center in ten or fifteen minutes. I told my wife that she should prepare some refreshments for between ten and fifteen people.

The Secretary arrived within fifteen minutes, but along with the two carloads I had expected were eight more carloads, making a total of over fifty people in the party. I wondered in passing, as I showed the Secretary over the Center, how the girls would make out for refreshments. Boldly I invited the Secretary and those around him into the dining hall for a snack. Imagine my amazement when I saw a table spread with all sorts of cookies and cake as well as glasses filled to the brim with juice, ice cubes and all — more than enough for everyone in the Secretary's party and our members besides. Those people walked in and enjoyed themselves.

I still have not quite gotten over the way it all worked out. Word spread and each one asked the other, "What can I do?" This one had glasses, the other one had juice, someone else had some cookies, another person had a cake prepared for other purposes, someone else had ice cubes, and so on; all converged with the needed resources and in the fifteen to twenty minutes available had everything prepared.

During this last month Dick Elkins has been going to various language areas checking translations. He has been helping the translators be sure that the material is idiomatic and accurate. Not long ago, we were holding a linguistic workshop to help different teams with their linguistic problems. Just yesterday we were working over a primer that had been sent in from the Bilaan area. Every day our radio technicians, teachers for the children, and house parents contribute to the basic job. Only teamwork will make translation possible. A very important part of this teamwork is the prayer help by those at home. No one person can produce a translation by himself. He may need help from an expert in the original languages of Scripture, or from one who has had extra training in linguistics, or from someone who can draw the pictures for a primer. All need the Lord's help in doing the job.

Just as my wife would not have been able to provide refreshments for the Secretary of Agriculture and his party by herself, so we depend on each other and upon prayer support at home to accomplish the task. Working together, we will be able to provide quickly and efficiently the Bread of Life to the mountain peoples of the Philippines.

Howard McKaughan
Director, Philippine Branch 1960

Love in Shoe Leather

I promised that I would give you a resumé of the opportunities that Madeline and I have had in providing service of love and "helps" to members of the diplomatic community here in Washington, D.C. The following are some of them:

—Took a pot of flowers to the chancery of an embassy to welcome a newly arriving Ambassador into our country.

—Helped an Asian, a close friend of an embassy member, with red tape about his immigration and visa problems.

—Helped the wife of an attaché locate the best college in the area in which to take courses in her speciality; also tried getting a scholarship for her but was unsuccessful.

—Escorted four different Ambassadors to North Carolina at different times to visit with Elaine and Uncle Cam; for one of these I organized a special tour in Raleigh, the state capital, and a recognition dinner through the Governor's office.

—Had the privilege of escorting Uncle Cam on several occasions as he made the rounds of the embassies and "the Hill" here in Washington, D.C.

—Gave sacks of freshly imported Florida oranges and grapefruit one winter to several Ambassadors and other diplomat friends.

—Had meetings and discussions with various cultural officers to discuss folklore, linguistics and ethnology of their respective countries and ways we can get some of that information on a broader base here in our country.

— Worked on getting a diplomat's brother to the U.S. for surgery which he could not get in Asia. But he died before we had the funding completed.

— Called several times with fruit and flowers for an Ambassador who had surgery in the Georgetown University hospital.

— Helped find a gynecologist for the wife of a diplomat.

— Arranged a week-end place to stay with the Howard McKaughans in Honolulu for a U.N. diplomat arriving in Hawaii from here, needing friends and a place to stay.

— Arranged with an embassy for a youth choir from Akron, Ohio, to tour the embassy and present the key to the city from the Mayor. The choir sang a lovely number for the staff of the embassy at their request during the tour.

— Took a diplomat and his aide deer hunting in Virginia.

— Arranged for an emergency appointment and then took a diplomat's wife (accompanied by one of her lady friends) to the dentist one morning when her husband was tied up in meetings at the State Department.

— Tried to get a magazine to permit the King of an Asian country to write a column for their bicentennial issue, but it declined.

— Worked on getting a way to show an excellent wild-life film of an Asian country on local TV but was not successful because of lack of enough time.

— Investigated at the request of an embassy the security and rooming facilities at the Cleveland Clinic for a ranking member of a royal family and entourage coming for medical work. I submitted my recommendations; and, as far as I know, they were followed to the letter.

—Served as a catalyst to organize and set up a luncheon in one of the embassies for one of the leading developers from Dallas, Texas, who was in town at the invitation of Cyrus Vance and who was making a trip to Asia. (The Ambassador's limo broke down about that time, so they asked me to go to the State Department to pick up the distinguished guests in our station wagon! Whew!)

—Gave a gift to the new-born son of a ranking diplomat.

—Watched over the family of a diplomat while he was abroad in his country on business. (While he was gone we had a blizzard, and their little girl had a wall mirror drop on her toe and break the toe.)

—Helped get information together on where to get the best buys on furniture for redecorating a diplomat's living room.

—Helped a diplomat's family repair their large, fancy dining room table and chairs that had not been assembled properly when imported from their country.

—Helped an embassy staff try to find a market for rugs woven in their country.

—Helped a diplomat's family get ladders for their servants to do some interior redecorating.

—Helped get information at the request of an embassy staff to try tracking down a girl from their country who had come here on a college scholarship and eloped with an American boy.

—Served as liaison in getting a rebuttal written for one of the Latin American embassies in response to a derogatory article written in *Newsweek*.

— Sent out congratulations to various embassies on the occasion of their respective National Days.

— Compiled a list of funding agencies interested in Asia for a Minister of Finance who came to Washington, D.C.

— Paid our respects to an embassy when one of their leaders died.

— On two occasions we had leaders from an Asian country in our home as guests, and we arranged for them to get together with some of their embassy folk.

— Played host one Sunday to the Deputy Permanent Representative to the U.N. from one of the Asian countries. He was in Washington, D.C., for the weekend.

— Entertained the head of the university of one of the countries where we are working and under whose auspices we operate in that land. He was with us as a house guest for three days and even went along to church with us on Sunday.

— Helped locate a suitable nursery school for one of the children of a diplomat.

— Stopped in at the U.N. in New York to pay a courtesy call on the staff of one of the Asian countries where we worked.

— Set up a meeting with three American business leaders and the commercial attaché of a Latin American embassy for discussions of potential investments in that country.

— On several occasions took reports from various branches to their respective embassies and Ambassadors.

— Helped to get a national language course to several embassy officials who badly needed them.

— Made efforts to have the course re-published, but to no avail.

—Researched and compiled a bibliography and some theoretical materials for an African embassy official on colloquial Arabic dialects in Africa.

—Worked with and for the U.S.-China Peoples Friendship Association trying to gain status and recognition so that I could get an invitation for me or someone in SIL to go to the People's Republic of China. I was successful in getting that invitation.

—Took a ranking diplomat and his wife along with me to Ohio where I spoke at a businessmen's meeting. I gave them a tour of Amish country which they enjoyed immensely.

—Had a diplomat and family in for dinner one evening when we learned that their cook was on vacation.

—Borrowed that cook one evening and had him cook a native meal for an Arlington County school teacher whom we invited.

—Worked with an African embassy at their request to help find a consultant on heavy equipment which six business men from their country needed. We were successful.

—At the request of an African embassy, I called on two lumber company officials when I was in Washington-Oregon to see if they would be interested in timber harvesting concessions in their land.

—Arranged for a youth group from a WBT supporting church in Ohio to tour an African embassy, hear lectures on that country and see displays of their artifacts, etc.

—Met at the request of an African embassy with one of their government officials one Saturday afternoon in his hotel when he spent a weekend here in Washington. I took him to the airport to see him off the next afternoon.

—Tried to help an Asian diplomat find employment after he had resigned from his post at the embassy for political reasons.

—Discussed with one of their diplomats ways and means for funding a clinic for an association for the blind, and other services in an Asian country.

—Attended a variety of social events—parties, dinner and receptions on Embassy Row and other places through these involvements.

There are trade secrets, as there are in most involvements. But there is no substitute for kind, loving, sincere attitudes of service. Trust has to be built into relationships, and that trust has to be earned. We look at these opportunities to be of service as from the Lord because we have not done a lot of soliciting for attention or recognition. It seems that the Lord has brought them along, and we have taken advantage of them as they have come. We are deeply grateful to Clarence Church, who has given us encouragement, even though this has cut deeply into our major assignment time. Thank you, Bud, for your interest.

Les Troyer
December, 1978

Ourselves,
Your Servants

One of the basic Wycliffe principles is SERVICE. God has blessed our basic principles and we should stick to them. You may say, "Oh, oh, social service! We've been warned against that. We've been sent to proclaim the Good News. But service, that's what the liberal missions are doing. They start hospitals and schools, and carry on agricultural programs. Wycliffe is not getting tied up in that, is it?"

II Corinthians 4:5 is the verse I like to urge on every one in the organization, especially recruits. It says: "We preach not ourselves, but Christ Jesus the Lord, and ourselves, your servants for Jesus' sake." Ourselves your servants for Jesus' sake! So I feel that we must serve. I realize that service activities are not the essentials, but the Lord spent a great deal of His time healing the sick, opening the eyes of the blind, helping people. And if He did it, and if Paul says that He did it and that we are to do it, I think we'd better do it, especially when we find that service opens doors. I do not know how we would get into countries where the doors are closed were it not for our vision of service, practically applied.

The Proper Umbrella

We do not do it as some missions do social service; the way some go about it, it appears to the nationals to be competitive. They say, "Look at that great big hospital run by foreigners. Foreign enterprise, foreign interest,

Ourselves, Your Servants **131**

foreigners coming to take over the country. It has been there for 50 years and it is still operating. Oh, it's nice when you need a doctor to find one there, but it is foreign." No, we do our service under the governments; at least, that is the policy. Of course, it is very easy to get away from that. If you start a literacy project in your language group, for instance, and do not put it under government supervision, you are in danger of being looked upon as a competitor by the nationalistic forces in that country.

So right from the start we put our program under the Ministry of Education, under the Ministry of Labor (because the Secretary of Labor in Mexico at that time was an Indian and interested in our program), and under the national university, especially for the linguistic research, so that they could point with pride and say, "See what we are doing out there among those Aztecs. We are doing it with the help of the Summer Institute of Linguistics." And that changes the situation completely. There is no longer jealousy. Instead they are proud of what we are doing — it is theirs.

When I planted a garden in the central square in the village of Tetelcingo, the garden which God used for opening up Mexico, for winning the heart of President Cardenas, who backed us there for 35 years, that garden was under the Mayor of the town. I said to him, "Mr. Mayor, I want to help you. I happen to know how to raise vegetables, and your people need to learn how to raise vegetables. We will work together."

Then when we needed some trees, it was the Mayor who got the credit because he was in charge of that garden and proud of it. When the President of the republic came down and saw what was being done, he saw that the people were learning — it was their project. When we needed money (because the Indians did not have money, and I did not have any either) I went to the Director of Rural Education, a man who at one time told me: "Townsend, if you do not quit trying to convert me, we will not be friends any more!"

I went to him and said, "Professor (he was one of the outstanding authorities on the history of modern Mexico), we want to plant trees in the central square of Tetelcingo. Fruit trees — avocados and citrus — and shade trees, and we need some money to buy them. Would you help out?"

You know, he felt proud! He did not have much money, but he pulled out five dollars and handed it to me. "Yes, sir, I'll help you." From then on he felt as though that project was his as well as ours.

The same was true with the Secretary of Labor. I went to him and said, "That town needs a road so that trucks can get into and out of it. You cannot get a truck in now and there is no way to get the Indians to work on a road. They say, 'Why, we are not doing anything that needs a truck. Why should we build a truck road?' If you will give them a truck, they'll say, 'Let's make a road so we can bring it into our town and use it.' "

The secretary caught the point and said, "Fine, we will provide the truck." I could have written to the States to Mr. Legters recommending that he raise $200 to buy an old used truck and give it to these Indians. But it would not have been worth a quarter of what this other truck was worth to our cause. This one that was given was an old, broken-down truck, worth perhaps $200, but it was donated by the Secretary of Labor. So, from then on, it was his project, too. The university felt the same way. That feeling is very, very important!

At one time we had a contract with the air force of Peru. We operated under them and our problems with the government were minimal in those days because it was their show. Then something happened and the contract with the air force was cancelled. After that we had numerous problems with the air force.

Help Us!

This matter of tying in locally is something we need to remember constantly. If there is no way of tying in closely by contract or by something similar, I would go to them and tell them that we need their help. "Help us!" Admit your problems and say, "We've got to have your help. How do you expect us, a bunch of foreigners, to get along out there in the jungle without your help? We must have your help." You may be sure they will give it.

Now, whether it is in literacy or aviation or radio, their help naturally will be limited. Sometimes you spend so much energy and time trying to get the funds that have been designated by the ministry for your literacy program that you wish you could operate independently. But do not do it!

And it is not only for SIL that this works. Some other expatriates find ways of doing it too. It's more difficult for some of them because they are sectarian in their approach. Some do not mean to be, but it turns out that way. One grand old pioneer in the Peruvian jungles said, "Uncle Cam, when I have to deal with a government official, I scratch my brain to figure out something he can do for me. Then I go and say, 'I need your help. Will you help me do this?' They are kind-hearted and enjoy helping a gringo who they always thought did not need any help. From then on I get along fine with the official."

What kind of service can we render in the USSR where the linguistic research has been done (as far as the diplomats are concerned — the officials who grant us permission to go)? Everyone knows how to read. You cannot help on a communal farm, and you do not have time to go out and be a shepherd—you would not get anything else done. So what kind of help can you perform? Well, we offered help to try to build international good will. And it appealed to them.

It appeals to other countries, too. When we went to Mexico, there was ill will toward the United States. It was apparent. When I first went to Mexico in 1920, it was very noticeable. And misunderstandings between our countries continued until Ambassador Morrow came and began to get things straightened out. Ambassador Josephus Daniels continued that good work. And Roosevelt cooperated beautifully, so that when Roosevelt died they put flags at half-mast and cancelled all the picture shows, dances and parties for three days in mourning for a Yankee President! It seems incredible. But he had done a great deal to break down ill will between our countries.

When we came down to do linguistic research, we had a few rules. One was never to write back home in a depreciating way concerning Mexico. Never talk about "the land of mañana." So many gringos do that. Never write home about the trains being late or about other things that Americans look upon as signs of backwardness. Instead, write back about their desire for progress, for friendship, their courtesies to us. On the whole, I think, our group the world over continues this policy of trying to build better esteem in the U.S. for the lands where we are working.

Out You Go!

There was a decisive event three years after we began in Mexico, when the attitude of foreigners was severely tested. It was the expropriation of the oil companies. Just three weeks before the expropriation decree was signed and published, President and Mrs. Cardenas came down to our Aztec village and, without saying it in so many words, told us of the problems with the oil companies. We had heard of some of them through the American Ambassador, Josephus Daniels.

After the expropriation, the oil companies began a tremendous campaign in the U.S. with articles in magazines and newspapers which were not telling the whole truth — only their side of the story and not the other side. I told Ambassador Daniels, who was a dedicated Christian man, that I was praying that the oil companies would not be able to sow permanent discord between the people of Mexico and the people of the United States. He said, "Townsend, you might as well pray for the devil as pray for the oil companies." He named one of them.

So I made a special effort to convince that company in New York, but they said, "No, we are going ahead and fight it out on the same basis as before."

We felt, therefore, that it was our duty to tell in the U.S. what we had observed — the disobedience of the oil companies, their refusal to submit to the decision of the Mexican Supreme Court, and matters concerning their labor problems. We did so. We made it known. We lectured in a number of places, including the University Club in New York's Empire State Building. It was my privilege to lecture there to a group which included three college presidents. When I got through, one man got up and said, "Townsend, you failed to say that they were not going to pay anything for the properties."

I said, "Well, sir, that's one of the details which has not been published. Actually, women in Mexico have brought their jewelry — Indians and peasants have brought turkeys and lambs as their contribution toward the fund to repay the oil companies. They will certainly pay when it is established with justice what the price is."

We gave out information to as many people as we could. We could not do it in an extensive way, but Mexico appreciated what we did do. I published a book called *The Truth about Mexico's Oil* and sent it to Congressmen in Washington. We can win the appreciation of these countries if we try to do what we are able in explaining how they want to be friends in spite of problems which need to be solved.

Choose Ye This Day....

Now, a word about service on the part of JAARS. Its full name is Jungle Aviation and Radio Service. The JAARS people hold a mighty key to helping the whole program because they get around.

If you are a pilot and fly over the home of an influential colonist on a lonesome river and never stop to say Howdy, to drink a glass of lemonade at his table, or eat a meal with him, or take mail out to him, or bring him out if he needs to go some place – if you never stop to show him a certain amount of courtesy, attention and respect, do not be surprised if, when he is elected senator from your area, he is not very friendly toward you.

But if you do stop and serve him, you are going to reap a benefit in many ways, even though you teach the Indians to read when he wants to keep them in ignorance so they will continue serving him. He will say, "They are teaching these Indians to read and getting some of them educated so they will not work for me as cheaply as they used to; nevertheless, that pilot is a very nice guy; I sure like for him to come by. He has taken me out once or twice, and he took my sick kid out to the hospital. They are all right, those pilots. I will do anything I can for them even though their colleagues are spoiling my employees."

Service! We have been criticized greatly because we serve monks and nuns. The editor of a big magazine which was, at one time, quite influential in the Christian circles from which most of our recruits came was very critical of the fact that we not only transported monks and nuns, but sought opportunities to do so — to wet the gunpowder of the ones who attacked us. He was not thinking about that, of course. He just said, "They are helping the Catholic Church; thus they are propagating false doctrines. That is wrong."

I talked to him and said, "Phil, let me give you a problem and you give me the solution: You are driving along a lonesome highway in Death Valley in California in the days when Death Valley was not visited by very many people as it is now. There is no food or water anywhere along this road, and you come to a broken-down bus. The driver looks like he's a rounder, just waiting to get to town to get drunk. One passenger is a priest headed for the next town to give a message against Protestantism. The other man is a Gideon and is anxious to get to town to give his testimony at the Presbyterian church. What are you going to do? You have room for three men in your car. Will you pick up all three and take them to safety or will you take only the Gideon and tell the rounder, 'I am not going to take you and thus help you get drunk; you stay here'? Of course, you must realize that if you don't take him, he may die for lack of water. Is that better than getting drunk? Or would you take the bus driver and the Gideon and leave the priest? You could say to him, 'You want to get to that town and give a message against Martin Luther and all his followers. I do not want to have any part in it, so I am going to leave you out here.' Or would you pick up all three of them, put the priest up beside you in the front seat, put the fellow who is anxious to get drunk beside the Gideon in the back seat, and drive on to town?"

My friend, brilliant editor that he was, replied that he would wait until God put him in such a situation and then he felt God would lead him. I replied that God had already put us in such a situation, that God had already led us, and that we work hard at it so that the priest in the seat beside me will be mellowed in his attack from the pulpit when he gets to town, and the bus driver beside the Gideon (I am pretty sure) will be led to Christ by the Gideon and will not get drunk.

I tell people who want to criticize us or who have been affected by criticism, "Do you think our pilots can submit would-be passengers to a doctrinal examination before taking them on board? Should they ask questions like, 'Can you sign this doctrinal statement? Are you evangelical, or are you Catholic? Or don't you believe at all?' After that, should he say, 'You qualify and you can ride in our plane since you are a good evangelical. But you, sir, are a Catholic; you can not. And you, sir, are a bum; I will not take you.' "

I said to my friend, "It is ridiculous. A pilot can not do all that; he has to serve everyone he can, regardless of his doctrines or attitudes. Folks can have their doctrine affected if a ride in a plane is at stake. It is very easy for them to say, 'I believe that and that.' And then get on the plane — acting out a farce."

Make the River Grind Your Wheat.

Service to all! Service in love, service in the name of Jesus Christ. Service to the enemy. The Old Testament makes it plain that a man was supposed to help his enemy by returning a stray ox. Christ said in Luke 6:27: "Do good to those who hate you." It is basic.

Stan Ford was one of our pioneers in Mexico. We

sent him out to a town where the people had to go a day's journey to get to a mill to grind their wheat. If they had to wait, it meant a day to get there and a day to return — three days to get a sack of wheat ground into flour. Stan Ford knew a bit about mechanics, so he said to them, "Why don't you have the river grind your wheat into flour?"

"The river? How can the river do that?"

He told them how. They liked the idea and asked what it would cost.

Stan wrote to me in Mexico City. I went to the electrical commission of the government and said, "Would you like to help an Indian town?"

"Why, yes," they said, "that's what we are established for."

"Well, they need a water wheel. Can you get them one?"

They gave me the data and the price. I wrote the information to Stan. He got the people together and told them. They said, "Is that all it will cost? Why, we spend that much money every time we hold a feast for St. Anthony! We will let the saint go without a festival this year so we can use the money to get a wheel and a mill." Soon they were grinding their wheat at home, eliminating the loss of three days and the charge for grinding.

Then Stan asked them, "Why don't you have chairs and tables instead of squatting on logs on the floor?"

They said, "It's a lot of work to saw trees into boards."

Stan said, "Why don't you let the river do it?"

"Can the river saw trees into lumber?"

"Sure it can."

So they let some other saint go without a festival and used the money to buy a saw mill big enough to supply them with boards to make tables and chairs.

Then Stan said, "Why are you in the dark all the time with just those little candles? Why don't you have electric lights?"

They said, "Electric lights? Why, only Oaxaca City, the capital, has electric lights! How can we have electric lights? We can not afford it."

Stan said, "Let the river do it."

They were convinced by now that the river could do things, so they let another saint go without a festival and bought a hydro-electric plant through the electrical commission.

Then the priest called them in. He said, "Do you know that that foreigner is a heretic? He has not attended any of our church services since he has been here. He has not come to mass a single time. Get him out of here!"

The Indians said, "Father, he may be a heretic, but he is the only one who knows how to fix our machinery. He stays!"

Yes, SERVICE! Service in the name of Jesus Christ will open doors. We serve through literacy, working through the government. We serve through linguistics, loaning teachers to universities and to institutes which want to offer linguistic courses. We serve through medicine insofar as linguists can.

God really uses service.

                                        W. C. Townsend

O King,
Live Forever

"The powers that be are ordained by God." How can that be? It is preposterous! "How," some ask, "can Hindu, Muslim, Buddhist, Communist or atheist powers be ordained by God?"

Does Paul's statement mean that God ordained both the Pharaoh who knew Joseph and the Pharaoh who knew him not? It means just that. The first was ordained by God to save the lives of God's people through Joseph. The second was ordained by God as one upon whom God's power would be shown as a testimony to God's name throughout the whole earth (Exodus 9:16; Romans 9:17).

Kay and I were married in 1936, and spent our first year together in El Paso, Texas, on the Mexico border. We had never heard of Cameron Townsend. And all we knew about Mexico was what we read in the El Paso papers. That was not flattering, to put it mildly. In fact, because all churches had been closed, the newspapers were printing very alarming stories, painting Mexico as being second only to the USSR in its far-left position. It is probably just as well that we did not know Townsend in those days. He was defending Cardenas, and nearly all that the American papers said about Cardenas was bad. His excellent qualities were not yet clear at all to most Americans. But Townsend had met him and was deeply impressed. Never one to shy from the fray, he wrote a pamphlet, "The Truth about Mexico's Oil," in Cardenas' defense when nearly every other American writer was attacking him.

In the summer of 1940 we met the Townsends, and by the late fall of that year we settled in Tetelcingo, where we saw quite a bit of them. Some time after our arrival I asked Mr. Townsend if it might be wise to try to meet a certain influential man (whom I named) in the hope that he would help us. "We do not 'try' to meet influential people," he replied. "But when God brings them our way and/or gives providential encounters with them, we try to be faithful friends."

I could see this in practice, as he sought to be a faithful friend to Cardenas. Nor was it a one-way street. He was not simply "using" Cardenas for what he could get out of him; he was seeking to give help also.

In 1976 I had the privilege of attending a dinner at which President Cardenas' widow was installed as President of the Patronato which sponsors SIL in Mexico. As I witnessed the strong affection, not only between the Townsends and Mrs. Cardenas, but also between them and innumerable other intimate Mexican friends, I could see the sweet fruit of 40 years being borne. It was very moving indeed.

Nor was it an empty gesture. It came at a time when our work worldwide had been under attack as never before. In at least four of the countries where we work there had been close-down threats or orders—all within the space of a few months. And many of those countries watch Mexico closely because it is a leader in the Third World.

But isn't it a misuse of an administrator's time to be doing things for unbelieving heads of state rather than for the members of the organization to which we belong? Daniel no doubt did a great deal for Shadrach, Meshach and Abednego. But he surely gave his first attention to King Nebuchadnezzar and to the King's successors. In fact, his devotion to them was so deep and firm that when King Darius, who had thrown him to the lions, asked if his God had been able to deliver him, Daniel's immediate words were, "O King, live for ever!" Was he honest? Should he not, if he were truthful, have replied, "I am safe, Mr. King, but no thanks to you"?

The salvation from famine which Joseph was able to provide for his father and brothers was not achieved by giving them his undivided attention. It came as a result of his loyal service to the "heathen" King of Egypt.

Jesus Himself, when asked if it was right to pay taxes to the foreign Emperor who was governing the Jewish people, said, "Render therefore to all their dues: tribute to whom tribute is due; custom to whom custom; fear to whom fear; honour to whom honour." (Romans 13:7) There are many Christians who would like to do Bible translation in countries which are not their own without rendering to the government authorities of those countries the recognition which is their due. No way. Or, as they say in Papua New Guinea, "No got!"

The Peacock Block

Jim Dean, Bill Oates and I were surveying the languages of Papua New Guinea in order to determine whether SIL should seek to work there. On our way we met a district officer who recommended we consider establishing headquarters on a piece of property known as the "Peacock Block" because a man by that name had once planned to grow coffee there. It seemed so ideal that we replied to the D.O. that we would like to lease it. Would he help us? He would and did.

But he was a Catholic and we were Protestants. That made no difference to him. He rolled up his sleeves and did what we needed in a wonderful way. Too many persons, however, fancy that the main hope of being allowed to do Bible translation in a given country lies with the Protestant officials in the country. It is not so. Not only the "powers that be" but also their rank in their hierarchy are ordained by God. And a part of what God has ordained in our day is that, in relations with expatriates, at least, the State is over the Church. It is a serious mistake, therefore, for expatriates to seek from officials of national religious organizations, whatever their rank or denomination, the permission which the national government is the one to give. In this connection I should like to correct a translation of Proverbs 17:8 which has been elected by both the Good News Bible and the Living Bible. "A bribe," they both say, "works like magic." I feel sure that the word which they translated *bribe,* and which the King James translators say means *gift,* has reference to the kinds of sentimental gifts which, while having little financial value, show appreciation for the person to whom they are given and recognition of his status.

When the McKaughans and Pittmans first went to the Philippines, for example, we were all poor as church mice. Nothing but a direct revelation from God could show us what sort of gift was suitable for Ramon Magsaysay and his wife at that time. But the Lord gave the revelation! Kay and Bobie McKaughan had put together a delicious combination of papaya and pineapple into a jam which we promptly christened "papinya." The next time we called at the Magsaysay residence, the husband was not home, but his wife met us. We had nothing to offer but a small jar of papinya jam. But it was the perfect Proverbs 17:8 gift. It did not make them feel indebted to us but did give them a warm feeling for us.

His Royal Highness

Near the end of 1978 I wrote the reigning monarch of one of the few countries which still have such rulers, as follows:

"On the occasion of the start of the year 1979, we who appreciate and love the Kingdom of _____ and the Royal Family wish to convey to Your Majesty our warm greetings and sincere prayers for God's best blessing on you and on the wonderful people you represent."

Some time later I received the following reply:

"By Command of His Majesty _____ I have the pleasure to inform you that His Majesty is pleased to thank you for the greetings and best wishes sent on the occasion of New Year. His Majesty wishes to reciprocate the same to you."

It was signed by the personal secretary.

Peter's Opinion

A man as blunt and forthright as Peter might have been expected to speak his mind in no uncertain terms to the Roman officials who crucified his Lord and gave Peter himself a hard time. Let's ask him. "Peter, what is your opinion on this touchy subject of what our attitude should be to government authorities?"

"For the sake of the Lord submit yourselves to every human authority: to the Emperor, who is the supreme authority, and to the governors (e.g., Pontius Pilate!) who have been appointed by him to punish evildoers and to praise those who do good. For God wants you to silence the ignorant talk of foolish people by the good things you do...respect everyone, love your fellow believers, have reverence for God, and respect the Emperor." I Peter 2:13-17.

RSP

That Was Good Lettuce

"We preach Christ Jesus the Lord, and ourselves your servants for Jesus' sake." Let's give a complete message as Paul did. Jesus Christ, the Savior, yes. Ourselves, your servants, also, for Jesus' sake. As He served His fellowmen, so we also must serve.

An old missionary in South America once told me, "Cameron, if I had my life to live over again, I would seek some way to serve the people in a more practical way than I have done, along with my Bible teaching and preaching." Then he told of a city in Mexico where the Gospel had been proclaimed for fifty years. "But," he said, "there is no noticeable change in the community as a result of the preaching of the Gospel." Of course, there is a change when you see some people converted and giving up drunkenness, but he was referring to something that would be more visible.

Go See for Yourself.

We are told to let our light so shine before men that they may see our good works and glorify our Father which is in heaven. That is one reason why, in our work in Mexico, right from the start, we tried to demonstrate the power of the Gospel in a place which could be seen by government officials. The town of Tetelcingo was only an hour and a half from Mexico City. Officials could visit and see what was being done. They said, "This is what Mexico needs." In Peru they would never get far out to the outlying groups where most of our work was being done, but near by, yes. That is one reason why we loved to entertain officials from Lima at Yarinacocha.

One day one of our staunch friends in Lima, who is connected with the University of San Marcos and highly esteemed by everyone who knows her, went into the Ministry of Education building in Lima. She saw two or three congressmen standing off to one side, chatting among themselves. One of them, a communist news-paper writer, saw her and said, "Good morning! How are you this morning?"

She said, "Fine. How are you?"

"Fine. Where are you going?"

She replied, "I am going to visit my tribe."

"Your tribe? What do you mean?" She said, "Oh, my tribe is up on the fourteenth floor." You see, the Min-istry of Education has given our Institute half of the four-teenth floor for SIL main offices in Peru, rent free. "My tribe," she said, "is the Summer Institute of Linguistics.

"And you know, Congressman, I am amazed that some people who are brilliant, brainy, capable folks, will talk about things they do not know anything about." You see, the Congressman had criticized us on the floor of Congress a few days before and the newspapers had re-ported it.

The Congressman smiled and said, "To whom do you refer?"

She said, "To you and to what you said about the Summer Institute of Linguistics in Congress the other night. Why don't you inform yourself before you open your mouth?"

He said, "What would you suggest?"

"Well, I suggest that you go out to the jungle and see for yourself; see what the members of the Institute are doing."

"I would be happy to," he replied. "Can you arrange a trip?"

"Of course I can. Come up with me to the fourteenth floor." So she brought him up to our office.

Immediately, by radio contact from Lima over the Andes to the jungle, a visit was set up for this communistic Congressman. He came out, stayed in our home, and every day went out to some different tribe or area to see what we were doing. After breakfast I would hand him the Bible and say, "Congressman, would you mind reading this chapter?" (Possibly the fourteenth chapter of John or the twenty-sixth chapter of Acts. I would carefully select the chapter.) He has a very fine radio program and is an expert reader; in fact, he is the only person I have ever heard read extempore without a single mistake in punctuation or intonation—an amazing reader.

He would read that chapter to us. Then he would go out to see what we were doing. On one trip he went with the fellows who took a load of supplies to the Aguaruna school teachers on the headwaters of the Amazon—the Maranon—in the big Catalina which Mexico gave us. He saw these pilots, one of them a former major in the U.S. Air Force, unloading the freight, putting it in the canoes, taking it to the river banks and carrying it up to where our smaller planes could shuttle it on to places where the big Catalina could not land. He thought, "Well! If these foreigners are serving my Indians, I had better get busy and serve them too." And so he started carrying freight also. After five days he went back to Lima and gave a lecture more than an hour long, to a full house, at the Writers and Artists Club, praising the work of the Summer Institute of Linguistics. He had seen with his own eyes the service that we were performing.

Partnership Garden

When we wanted to work in Mexico I met a young man who had been born in Mexico of missionary parents, but even so had had to spend a thousand dollars and a year of effort waiting in ante-rooms, trying to see officials, and at times trying to avoid policemen, because he had been ordered out of the country once or twice. Finally, at the cost of a thousand dollars and the loss of a great deal of time, he got his permit to live in Mexico. I figured, "That will not work for us because we want to bring in several hundred linguists." As a matter of fact, we have taken more than three hundred linguistic researchers into Mexico. We have also sent many to the Philippines and Peru and elsewhere and they were welcome because they served.

So I raised lettuce down in Tetelcingo, and oh, how God blessed that lettuce patch! The ground was no good, but bats were living in old plantation manors which had been wrecked during the revolution; so the Indians went out and brought in the bat droppings for fertilizer and anything else that would fertilize our partnership garden. And the lettuce prospered remarkably. I would take beautiful heads to the home of the Director of Immigration with an explanatory note saying, "This is an experiment we are carrying on in this Aztec village trying to teach the Indians some gardening." We had planted various vegetables and fruit trees. We had planted them in the central square, not on private property but on town property. It was a town project, so that we were working in partnership with the government, not in competition with it.

Missions, however, if they carry on social service, generally do it in a way that nationalistic governments look on as competition. We do not. We go to the governments and say, "We are going to be studying these languages; we want to be of service to you while we do it. We know that you have a desire to raise the standard of living of these people. We need to be living out among them to learn their languages. We are at your orders. How can we be of help to you?"

They say, "My, what a strange bunch of Americans—wanting to help us! Generally the Americans come and tell us what we ought to do and what is wrong with us. This gang comes out and says, 'Can we be of service to you because we admire what you are doing for your people?' Why, sure we can use you!" So they welcome our on-the-spot cooperation, put us to work and are very appreciative. It is just the thing we want to do. The government's requests are like that of the Princess of Egypt asking Moses' mother to take care of baby Moses—it was the very thing she wanted to do. It is right down our alley.

So I left this lettuce and note at the home of the Chief of Immigration. Previously, Mr. Legters, Dr. Dale and I had waited weeks to see this man's predecessor and never did get to see him. The day after I delivered the lettuce to the new man, I stationed myself in the hallway of the approach to his office where he would pass by. Finally he came. "Good morning, Townsend."

"Good morning."

"By the way, Townsend, that lettuce was very fine; that was good lettuce. Come on in." Then he took me in by the inner door so I did not have to go through the waiting room. Then we sat and talked about lettuce, and about the Indians' need of learning how to eat vegetables instead of just eating tortillas and beans.

Finally he said, "By the way, Townsend, is there anything I can do for you?"

"Well, we would like to bring in five new linguists; can you sign these permits?" Of course he signed them. I found it much easier, much more pleasant, to approach the problem that way, through the gateway of service.

Well, as we worked in that garden, every little while we would take out the New Testament, sit down, and read it to the Aztec Mayor. Then he would explain it to his fellow-men in the Aztec language. One day he came and said, "Professor, what has happened to me anyhow? Since I have been reading that book you loaned me, I cannot do the bad things I previously did because that book stops me." And he had been a "rounder"! He had served in Zapata's army and in the Federal army; the wife he had was number 28; he would fight with one, they would separate, and he would get another. But he married the last one and has lived with her for 25 years. He became a wonderful preacher of the Gospel. He gave up marijuana; he gave up drunkenness; he quit toting a gun to kill his enemies — transformed by this Book which he studied when not at work on the garden or occupied in other ways.

Win Hearts through Friendship.

We Americans have attained a prominence which makes us a world power, but we do not know how to use that position of prominence correctly. I wish that there would be a revival of a spirit of service to the world on the part of the United States. There is so much we should do for the world. We try to do it with money; we vote billions for foreign aid, and we think we are helping the world. But what the world is looking for is the spirit of service in our people who go abroad. That the world seldom sees, except in missionaries. But missionary service, so often, is carried out in a partisan, denominational way which is not appreciated by officials. When an American goes to a country and seems to have an axe to grind, the service he may perform is not looked upon as real service.

I was riding once with a professor whom the President of Mexico had assigned to help us in Tetelcingo, and I saw a cross. I said, "Professor, that cross reminds me of a hymn which was written by a British consul on an island off the coast of China when he saw a cross still standing where a Portuguese church had burned down." Then I quoted part of the hymn to him.

He said, "Don't talk to me about that; you are just like my old uncle, the Archbishop of Chihuahua, always trying to win somebody to your organization."

I said, "Wait a minute, Professor; I did not say anything about an organization. I just mentioned my best Friend, and I want you to know my best Friend. The Lord Jesus Christ saved me; He keeps me; He's my joy in life; He's my hope; He's my stay. He's everything to me, and He's not an organization. He is my best Friend."

If service can be performed without sectarianism, how good it is! A Christian businessman came down to Peru after a big disaster and donated some money. Everyone was contributing. Some people had been burned out of their homes. He said, "I will give money but it has to go through the Protestant church."

"Oh, is that your attitude?" they replied. "You will help people who believe the way you do, but you will not help others?" So they did not appreciate his offer.

Some of our linguists thought we ought to limit the use of our donation the same way. I said, "No. Let us send the money to the town officials. Let them use it wherever they feel it is needed. And then if we see that some of our brethren in Christ are neglected, let's do a little extra on a personal basis to help them."

America needs to know about these countries. A service which we can perform is to let our fellow citizens of the United States and Canada and other "developed" countries know what these underdeveloped countries are doing.

Never put anything derogatory in your prayer letters, dear ones. I used to talk about the "land of mañana." I do not do that any more. I talk about the lands of friends, because that is what they are. Friendship goes a long way in Latin America, in the Philippines, and in any part of the world. Win the heart of a Latin American through friendship, and he will take the shirt off his back to give to you when you need it. When we go down there and see the need, we should write back and let our friends know how the United States should be helping.

Why Write a Book?

One thing I wanted to do was to let the United States and Canada know about General Cardenas. I had observed him in action, working 16 hours a day to help his people, always out among poor people, seldom inviting the high and mighty. He even invited a group of us unknown Bible translators, back in October 1936, to the castle of Chapultepec to dine with him. I decided that I should take time to write a book about him. It took a lot of research. From 1937 to 1952 I must have spent time totalling over a year gathering information and writing *Lazaro Cardenas, Mexican Democrat.*

You say, "What's a Bible translator doing writing a book, a secular book, about a Latin American statesman?" Well, I thought it was my duty to the people of the United States to let them know what was going on down there. And General Cardenas' help to our linguists saved us many years of work on customary red tape and assisted in other ways. Thus I owed it to him as well as to the people of the United States.

Dr. Pittman gave a copy of the book to Ramon Magsaysay, who became President of the Philippines. At that time he was Minister of Defense. He called Dr. Pittman on the phone at the University of Pennsylvania and thanked him for the book. He said that indirectly it had been a great help to his people. Later I learned that my book had become President Magsaysay's favorite book next to the Bible. I was told by one of his aides — a Major who was with him constantly up to the time of his death — that it had changed the course of history in the Philippines because Magsaysay endeavoured to help the common people as Cardenas did in Mexico and had great success in doing it.

Then, when Dr. Pittman led a large group of SIL members to the Philippines, Magsaysay simply told the officials, "Help Pittman and his group."

When the officials knew that President Magsaysay wanted the Summer Institute of Linguistics to be working in the Philippines, they said, "All right. We do not know just how the law can classify a large group of Americans coming in all at once, but we will find a way." They discovered that, on recommendation of the President, the law permitted them to give temporary permits to our members. So they said, "We will give you 'temporary' permits, good for ten years; when the ten years are up, come around and get renewals."

When it was necessary to use radios, President Magsaysay was no longer on the scene. A tragic accident had taken his life, but the officials told our director, Dr. McKaughan, that whatever President Magsaysay had promised, they would do. "And you shall have radio communication. Just donate those radios to the Philippine Signal Corps, and it will return them to you with orders to operate them." And so we are operating radios in the Philippines today to safeguard the health of our members and to make the work more efficient—under orders of the Philippine Signal Corps. Don't you see that service pays? Service will open every door.

"We preach not ourselves but Christ Jesus the Lord." And when Christ is lifted up, He draws all men unto Him. If you lift Him up in an unprejudiced way, lift Him up without trying to promote an organization; just lifting up Jesus Christ, the Saviour of mankind—and ourselves servants, humble servants, needy servants, intelligent servants, prepared servants, willing servants, for Jesus' sake—will open every door.

Cameron Townsend

Why Attend Government Social Functions?

Excerpts from a letter to a friend in Canada,
March 18, 1955:

"...you can assure him that wherever we go we take our Lord with us; we have had priceless opportunities to witness for our Savior in these functions to which he refers as 'questionable.' The very fact that at a President's banquet, for instance, we do not partake of alcoholic beverages is a loud testimony to all. One typical privilege was the opportunity at a government dinner to take the Minister of Education aside in the library while drinking and gaiety were going on in the other rooms and give him a careful explanation of how the love of Christ prompts our young people to go out among the Indian communities and translate the Scriptures for them."

"I suppose that some pious Jew may have been scandalized when he saw Shadrach, Meshach and Abednego enter the King's idol temple, and he may have dashed off to the synagogue to denounce the three men publicly. I used to wonder why they went instead of staying home and sending the King a message to the effect that they would not go to the affair; but now I realize that their testimony was much more effective when given right on the scene. The Lord set us the example of ministering to sinners and publicans (politicians), and to do it we have to go where they are."

Cameron Townsend

One Branch's Dinner Pattern

During the first part of 1980 we had four major evening dinners. These were held at our Brasilia Center. One was for federal congressmen, another for people in the news media, a third for diplomats, and the last for high government officials.

This is the procedure we follow for such occasions. As guests arrive they are shown through our Center: the linguistic and spiritual publications (Scripture portions in Indian languages), a map of tribal locations covering an area equal to the 48 adjacent states, the computers (and how they speed translations), our unique library (considered the best linguistic library in Brazil), and the department of graphic arts, including the print shop.

Supper is then served. After the supper our linguist/translators present a program designed to give an in-depth view of our work. We have found that the supper atmosphere is much more conducive to making friends than attempts to interview individuals in their busy offices.

Bob Schneider
July 1980

Come to the Picnic

July 4, 1939

Dear Friend:

The President of the Republic of Mexico, General Lazaro Cardenas, has kindly consented to be the guest of honor, together with his official staff, at an open air picnic which this institution has planned as an expression of gratitude for the great help and encouragement which he has extended our group of linguists and Bible translators now laboring among the Indian groups of his nation.

We have found in President Cardenas not only a very valuable friend but also a great inspiration because of his own sterling character and the way he gives himself unreservedly for the people, literally pouring himself out in their service with no thought of reward, not even of appreciation. We have been more than convinced of the truth of the statement of the Honorable Josephus Daniels, Ambassador of the United States in Mexico, that President Cardenas is "one of the most unusual men in the world, faced by one of the most difficult problems in the world." President Cardenas has observed with favor the self-sacrificing efforts of our young linguists to help the many Indian tribes in numerous ways, including that of giving them in their own languages portions of the greatest Book we have to offer them, the Bible, not with any sectarian finalities, but as a basic contribution to the solution of the problem which President Cardenas calls the greatest problem in the world, the human heart.

The visit of President Cardenas to lower California provides an opportunity for our friends in southern California to get to meet this great man, and so we take extraordinary pleasure in inviting you to the picnic. It will be held on Friday, the 7th of July, at one o'clock in the afternoon at the old Casino in Agua Caliente just south of Tijuana.

You may invite such of your friends as you know who hold toward Mexico the same attitude of good neighborliness and Christian service as we hold and who can appreciate President Cardenas' high ideals. Your Mexican friends will be particularly welcome. All who come should bring their own basket lunches and table service.

If you desire transportation by bus or on the Santa Fe R.R., or if you are going in your own auto and have room for extra passengers, please phone to the office of the Church of the Open Door in Los Angeles, Mr. Wm. G. Nyman, 1305 N. Louise St., Glendale, Calif., or Mr. Eugene Griset, Santa Ana, California.

Yours sincerely,
W. C. Townsend, Director

III

The High Cost
of Short Circuits

"For two months I was no longer accepted
as a friend by the fine men
who were by-passed by the short cut."

-Jose Estrella

We Did Not
Go Public

In November 1974 there was a special conference on linguistics covered by the papers. The opening paper was given by the most prominent linguist in Nepal; we were not aware of it ahead of time. It was a charge against both SIL and the university to the effect that we were doing nothing about training Nepali linguists. Another gentleman, who had other motives, took this as a base and published two full-page articles in the newspaper giving numerous false allegations about our linguistic work.

Rather than write a rebuttal for the local newspaper, I felt led to write an answer in private and give it to the Vice-Chancellor of the university. I told him that it was not our position to defend ourselves in the country but it was appropriate for him to do so. He agreed with this and sent my letter to the leading linguist, who was very happy for the clarification. When I subsequently talked to this linguist, privately, he asked me if I intended to publish my letter. I told him I did not, but that I wanted to clear the air. He said I was right, and that it was the responsibility of the university and not ours to defend SIL. Later this man became friendly and is still one of our best friends in Nepal.

One thing we did from the very beginning was to try to see government people to get their advice and follow it. When we were accused of being involved with the CIA, we went to the Vice-Chancellor and told him again it was not our place to defend ourselves. On that basis he wrote a letter to the magazine in question refuting the allegation. Also as a result of our behaviour to the government of Nepal, we received a thank-you letter from the office of His Majesty, which, I was told, was unprecedented.

Dick Hugoniot

Loaded Words

It comes as a surprise to most persons of European extraction to discover that many of the words he uses without a second thought are loaded when used in Asia.

People in that part of the world, for example, dislike intensely to be referred to as Asiatics or Orientals. But it is quite all right to refer to them as Asians.

When they are seeking to attract tourists, they, of course, use words like *Orient* or *Far East*, which sound exotic to tourists. But they do not appreciate the inference that the center of the earth is Europe or America as is implied by terms like *Orient* or *Far East*. They would prefer Asia, or specific country names.

Filipinos feel that referring to their country as the Philippine Islands makes it sound small or weak or fractured. They much prefer to call it "The Philippines." Filipino is also often spelled "Pilipino," but *never* "Philipino."

Officials of most countries dislike very much to hear a couple of foreigners refer to a language group as "our tribe" and its language as "our language." The word *tribe* itself is considered derogatory in some countries. "Cultural minority," "minority language group" or "cultural community" are usually better.

Certain religious terms are not appreciated in many countries of Asia. The designation "missionary" is especially disliked in a good many countries. Indirect reference to "other missionaries" may, by implication, classify a person with them.

The first person plural pronoun should not be used in reports. It often gives the impression of "first plural exclusive." That is, "This is the project of us foreigners but not of you nationals who read this report."

Even criticism of unspecified parties referred to only as "they," "them" or "it" can be interpreted as criticisms of the country and/or people of the country in which the criticism is heard.

The word *informant* is especially wrong to use. For very many people it is understood to mean *informer* or quisling.

The word *survey* is frightening to many because it raises the specter of spying.

Many words have a military sound: base, advance, occupy, strategy. However dynamic they may seem when used in home circles, they should not be used in host countries.

Any allusions or inferences which may seem to imply connections with intelligence agencies should be scrupulously avoided. Excessive interest in maps and map terminology can be suspect.

A "professional" interest in, or use of, political topics and terminology can make a person seem to be a government representative rather than a linguist. On the other hand, a person *should* be a professional in his ability to use linguistic and educational terms.

All terms which can be interpreted as racist should be avoided.

RSP

Shall We Blast
Our Hosts?

How to Fight against Bullfights

By the time Magsaysay had been President of the Philippines for a year, he had taken at least three initiatives which troubled me. He planned to reintroduce bullfights, a national lottery, and diplomatic relations with the Vatican, none of which had characterized the Philippines since the days when the country was a colony of Spain.

Fired up with fervor, I sat down and wrote him a letter, quoting Scripture.

That was certainly better than "going public" with an article denouncing him. But I erred badly by sending it to him through the mail. I should have carried it to him personally and given him a chance to object personally. He never refused our requests for an audience.

In spite of my foolishness in mailing instead of hand-carrying my letter of concern, the President wrote a very courteous acknowledgement. Then, to my astonishment, I observed that the plans for bull-fights and a national lottery were quietly scrapped, and the Ambassador to Italy was given responsibility for diplomatic relations with the Vatican. Best of all, communication with the President was not interrupted. We were allowed to continue working in the country and calling on him just as before.

Not long after this incident, our translators with one

of the Manobo groups reported that lowland settlers were taking land away from the Manobos. After attempting to make sure we had our facts straight, I took the matter up personally with the President the next time I saw him. "Get Congressman X (who represented that area) on the phone," said the President to an aide. An attempt was made on the spot. The call was not completed while we were in the office, but knowing Magsaysay's promptness in dealing with matters, I have no doubt it went through later. There was at least temporary relief for the Manobos in that location.

After Magsaysay's untimely death we needed to complete arrangements for starting JAARS work in the Philippines. The President had told us how to do it, but we were not yet off the ground at the time he lost his life in an airplane accident. So we took the matter to his Minister of Defense, through whom we had been told to work. "Just consider that Magsaysay has never died," the Minister advised us. It was his way of saying that the late President's instructions would be carried out as though he were still alive. And they were.

The Apostle Paul had to work under Emperor Nero, whose name is synonymous with greater repression than any of us have had acquaintance with. Given Paul's eloquence with the pen, it is significant that he neither launched a personal protest against Nero's oppression nor incited any of his colleagues or assistants to do so. On the contrary, he wrote to the believers in Rome (of all places!): "Everyone must obey state authorities, because no authority exists without God's permission, and the existing authorities have been put there by God. Whoever opposes the existing authority opposes what God has ordered; and anyone who does so will bring judgment on himself."

On one occasion in the Philippines there was a flurry of activity honoring Mary, which some interpreted as idolatry. I was both incensed and frustrated because I could not think how to fight it. Remembering Uncle Cam's advice, "The best way to fight the machine is to love the individual," I remembered an influential priest to whom I had promised some linguistic material. I took the material and called on him. I could tell from the course of our conversation that the Lord was working in his heart as well as in mine. I came away reassured that, in spite of my imaginings, God was doing things to right wrongs.

A Case of Mistaken Identity

When we first went to the Philippines, the Roman Catholics had an eloquent lay spokesman fluent in both English and Tagalog, a professor in the leading Catholic university.

Whenever there was a "holy war" to be fought, this man was out front, writing brilliant letters and articles promoting the Roman Catholic cause. By a fascinating "error," because of the similarity between his name and the name of another leading language expert, we started sending linguistic articles to the professor. By the time I discovered the mistake, the professor considered himself a friend, because of the mailings. When we asked for office space, we were given space in his office in the Department of Education. Several of us had tremendous witnessing privileges with him as a result. By the time he was dying of cancer, many years later, he was delighted to have us come to his home, read the Bible to him, and pray with him. I have no doubt that we will see him in heaven.

Now, when Billy Graham and other evangelists hold meetings in Manila, they frequently find themselves very well received in Catholic circles. Thousands of Catholics attend their meetings, often with the blessing of Catholic officials. Some will say we should have been denouncing those officials in the press and from platforms. God has told us that remonstrance with them should be personal and private. I did just that with the professor, quoting many Scripture warnings and commands against idolatry. He listened patiently and quietly to my long exhortation. I personally am convinced that it bore fruit in his life, and no doubt in others through him. His friendliness certainly mellowed my abrasiveness.

Theodore Roosevelt is quoted as saying, "If I must choose between righteousness and peace, I choose righteousness." The assumption that we must choose between righteousness and peace is an Old Testament dilemma. In Christ, "Mercy and truth have met together, righteousness and peace have kissed each other" (Psalm 85:10). And the Lord has showed us how to do it. The ground for sowing the seed of truth must be prepared by antecedent words and acts of mercy (lovingkindness, steadfast love, unfailing love). And Christians must learn to apply them in that order, whether in family, church, employment, or government relations. As we do so, we will no longer think in terms of public protest against host governments nor of denouncing oppressive rulers, but of ways to continue serving the cultural minorities in the lands which have so hospitably allowed us to do so. And changes for the better will take place.

One Bandage for One Wound

A couple of years ago, Christian friends of ours in New Jersey were being put through the wringer by neighbors whose teen-age boy tormented the children of our friends. They asked me if it was all right to call the police. "No," I said. "Perform acts of friendly neighborliness to the parents of the obnoxious boy and to the boy himself."

They said, "We have tried, but the parents are as bad as the boy. They indignantly reject all our overtures."

"Keep trying," I said. "Paul says that love never fails."

Perhaps a year later there was a sudden change. Our friends gave the offending boy a set of Narnia books. They told him they loved him. The hatchet was buried between the two families, and genuine peace, based not on police action, but on New Testament procedures, was established. You can hardly imagine a happier family than the one who tried the love route against their oppressor and found, finally, that it worked.

Tim and Barbara Friberg were in Phnom Penh almost up to the time that the government there was taken over by the Khmer Rouge. Refugees were flooding into the capital, the number of wounded was astronomical, and even herculean efforts seemed futile for feeding the countless thousands. Tim wrote, "We are often overwhelmed by a feeling of hopelessness and helplessness. It seems that there is nothing we can do. But we find that there are things we can do to minister to these people when we tackle them one at a time."

It is an extremely significant statement. Blasts in the media, demonstrations, protests, explosions of anger and indignation are not God's way. God gives each of us just one opportunity of ministry at a time: one cup of cold water for one thirsty child, one bandage for one wound, one half-hour to visit one dying friend. It is no use throwing our one little lunch away with a sarcastic "What good is this when 5000 are hungry?" It is even less use to blame the wicked landlords, the stingy employers, or the "insensitive" government. "Maturity is the state of mind reached by those who no longer blame others for their troubles," one profound observer has declared. The worst thing we can do for people we want to reach for Christ is to encourage them to blame someone else for their suffering. Only when we learn to look to Jesus alone for recourse and relief will we be giving the right kind of message and example to others whom we are trying to reach.

The Criticize-other-governments Game

Recently a very clever satire appeared in a popular magazine which publishes critical articles about national governments. The wrinkle of this particular article was that Moses should have been submissive to Pharaoh instead of leading Israel's rebellion against him. Of course, the author does not believe that. He was poking fun at Christians who advocate being submissive to governments. But there are at least three aspects of the life of Moses which this writer made no mention of: 1. What God did to Korah and 253 others who rebelled against Moses (Num. 16:1-40). 2. The fact that God chose Moses—the meekest of men—to lead His people, not in acts of violent struggle against the Egyptians, nor even in demonstrations or declarations of protest against Egyptian wickedness, but purely in an exodus, engineered by God, not by man. 3. The fact that God repeatedly accredited what Moses was doing by supernatural miracles. Any of us who would like to do something similar must think twice lest we be found as "sons of Sceva" (Acts 19:11-16).

Because of points of view such as those expressed in this magazine, some members recommend that we "back off from government contracts," feeling that we should have "freedom to criticize when criticism is needed" (meaning criticize our host governments). The problem is that freedom of a guest to criticize his host is counterproductive. It fails to produce the desired change in the host and it quickly results in the guest's becoming persona non grata.

Many Christians feel, as Peter did in the Garden of Gethsemane, that they should draw their sword and wade in to defend the Lord. Or that they should at least unsheathe a pen to defend Him. In my opinion, the Lord is still saying the same thing to us as He said to Peter: "Put up your sword (and your pen)."

Then Peter sulked, with his tragic denial as the final fruit.

But the Lord gave him a chance to demonstrate moral (instead of physical) courage by going to the home of Cornelius (representative of the Roman nation which crucified Christ) with the Gospel. And He called Paul to use his pen, not against, but for winning the same Romans.

Other Christians like to visualize themselves as Old Testament type prophets, called to pronounce doom on the nations of the world. But Christ called Wycliffe not to denounce governments but to announce good news. The world will never lack critics. But there is a great lack of those who, like Christ and the apostles, are willing to suffer in silence the cruelty and arrogance of the Roman Empire while speaking out boldly the good news of the Gospel. Even the beautiful words "We must obey God rather than man!" was not their way of saying "We must criticize the wicked government in obedience to God," but "We must spread the Good News instead of being silent or spreading Bad News."

RSP

He Rose to the Bait

The fish at Jungle Camp are notoriously hard to catch. At least, they were when I was there. Many an angler found himself hopelessly disappointed by the wary fish. But one day I found a log over a deep pool inhabited by a fine fish. And because the water was so clear, I could see everything that went on. Having found some attractive bait, I concealed the hook in it and dropped it right in front of the fish's nose. He was not interested. But I persisted. I made it dance. It shimmered in the crystal pool. Finally seduction worked. A quick flick – and I had him hooked.

There is a strange power in seduction. Even when it is recognized, it is often successful because the target fails to flee until it is too late.

Hezekiah was a winner. He followed the Lord faithfully, being courageous enough to destroy even the bronze serpent of Moses because the people were burning incense to it. And God repaid his loyalty with three impressive miracles – slaying 185,000 Assyrians plus their King Sennacherib, healing Hezekiah of a fatal illness, and making the shadow go back on the sundial.

No wonder he felt expansive when an admiring delegation arrived from Babylon. No doubt he praised the Lord publicly in their presence, finding it a great occasion to witness and keeping only a tiny bit of the glory for himself. But as their fawning and flattery persisted, and as he savored its sweetness, something else happened. No doubt he thought he was rising to the occasion. Alas, he was rising to the bait. Like a virgin seduced by a suitor, he uncovered everything. The lecherous eyes took it all in. Thoughts began. One day the erstwhile Babylonian admirers returned and took Hezekiah's people captive.

Josiah was another winner. He, too, followed the Lord with all his heart, ridding the land of the images, mediums, wizards and other abominations which had polluted it. For him Satan had another kind of bait — foolhardiness. Pharaoh's campaign against Assyria was no affair of his. But, flushed with spiritual victories, he felt invincible. On the plain of Megiddo an Egyptian arrow penetrated his disguise and felled him.

Moses' meekness no doubt made him feel immune to the dangers of anger. So when the people groused for the skaty-eighth time against him and the Lord, his guard was down. "Listen, you rebels!" he fired back, and the damage was done. Satan had successfully baited him, too.

Two favorite types of baiting catch expatriates. The first takes place overseas. A malcontent comes seeking help. The foreigner came to give help. So he rises to the occasion, lending a sympathetic ("therapeutic," he believes) ear. But the recital of the sufferer's woes gradually turns to blame of the powers-that-be. What began as a kindly listening to a friend in need ends with, "Yes, yes. I understand. It's too bad. There ought to be a law against it." And the conversation becomes not a confession of the speaker's sins but a claim of government wrongs.

The second type takes place when the expatriate returns home. He is now a hero. His admiring audience hangs on his words. In the question session they commiserate with him over his sufferings — unhygienic conditions, primitive people, demonic powers, unbelievably bad governments. And the words of the incautious traveller get back to the government of the land where he bad governments. And the words of the incautious traveller get back to the government of the land where he was a guest.

> "Come hither, hither, pretty fly,
> with the pearl and silver wing;
> Your robes are green and purple;
> there's a crest upon your head;
> Your eyes are like the diamond bright
> But mine are dull as lead..."
> You have the smartest crew abroad,
> The greatest mission band;
> You're anthropologically very correct —
> Strategically best in the land...

Most insidious of all is the temptation to betray your host. It is never suggested, of course, as a form of betrayal. The opening gambit is that you are an "authority" by virtue of your first-hand experiences in a foreign land. And it is suggested that providing information to your interrogator will "protect" your host from the sinister forces which would destroy him. But if the interrogator is an intelligence agent, you may very well become a potential or actual traitor to the people you came to serve.

A retired American Colonel was on his way to visit the CIA one day, and was tempted to take an SIL member with him. But then he decided against it because, as he explained to the SILer later, "If you give them (the CIA) intelligence information, you are a spy."

On another occasion, a friendly U.S. university official sent a CIA official to see the Director of an SIL at that university, "just in case the Director might have some information of interest for him." The Director courteously explained that he was trusted by the national

He also explained that the results of the SIL linguistic studies would be published for all to see and benefit. The CIA official accepted this polite refusal and did not press further for information.

But how can you know whether it is an intelligence agent questioning you? The best answer to that is to refuse permission to any SIL member to give political or military intelligence about any country, or any other type of information which could be used to endanger the security of a country. Each SILer should be obliged to maintain a firm position of not being qualified to report on political, military or intelligence matters.

A good many people who have been raised in "free speech" countries regard freedom of speech not only as a sacred right but even as an obligation. SIL members, however, have exactly the opposite obligation in their role as expatriate guests in countries not their own. The "privilege" of talking like an authority against countries they have visited or lived in as expatriates is not theirs. Does this sound too negative? Does it leave them nothing to say? Not at all. There are good bits of information about the people and culture of every country in the world which can be freely shared. If, in fact, the SILer loves people in the countries he goes to as he claims, he should make known to others the admirable qualities of the people he has seen.

RSP

Why Did Those Aliens Fail to Register?

I was looking for the Western Bukidnon Manobo on the island of Mindanao in the Philippines. I had been given the name of a Filipino pastor who knew them and knew where they lived. Travelling alone and by bus, I arrived in the small village where the pastor's home was. I was sure there would be no problem locating him; the village could not have housed more than a few hundred souls.

As the bus pulled up to a stop, I breathed a sigh of relief that I would soon be able to rest in the friendly shade of the pastor's house. But a warning inner voice checked me. "Not yet," it seemed to say. "Call on the Mayor first."

I had no idea who the Mayor was, where he lived, or whether he knew anything about the Manobos. And I was tired from the long bus trip. It was with some reluctance, therefore, that I asked a by-stander where I might find the Mayor. But the question was easily answered, and before long I was in the presence of the Mayor. I produced my credentials and stated the purpose of my trip — to locate the Manobos — not mentioning the pastor. "Oh," exclaimed the Mayor, "no problem. There is a man here who knows all about the Manobos. I will send a guide to take you to his house." The expert he referred to was the pastor I was seeking! I was guided to him by the Mayor's aide.

U.S. Passport Number 1234

For us who have grown up in countries of which we are citizens, it requires a major shifting of gears to learn how to work in countries where we are foreigners. One of the most crucial adjustments which has to be made is to learn the importance of giving continual recognition to the supreme authority of the government of the land in which we are guests.

Years ago I was the proud holder of U.S. passport number 1234. Not that I am that old. It was the 1,234th passport issued by the U.S. Embassy in Mexico. But — can you believe it? — I forgot the number.

We were crossing a wide Peruvian river in a dugout canoe. Only the regulation "two-finger width" separated the current from the gunwale of the canoe. And my passport was buried deep in the duffle bag at the bottom of the canoe.

We had just reached the far shore of the river when an official came running down the bank on the side we had left. "Who is that foreigner?" he shouted. I called my name back. "Where did he come from?" he asked. I gave my origin. "Where is he going?" I gave my destination. "He should have registered before crossing the river. All who cross must show their passports." My hosts shouted back explanations which partly satisfied the official. "All right," he agreed. "I'll let him go if he tells me his passport number."

Then my mind went blank. I cudgelled my brains trying to remember. "What in the world is my number?" I fretted. At last it came to me. I shouted back across the river: "Uno, dos, tres, cuatro!" I'll never know whether he believed me or gave up in despair. At any rate, he let us go.

Not every experience is so easily resolved, however,

as that of the passport in Peru. On my first arrival in Irian Jaya, seeking permission for SIL work there, I goofed more than once in relations with the government officials. The first mistake came when I went in to see the government secretary in Jayapura. Jim Baptista, Doug Hunt and Ken Wiggers were with me. The title "secretary," as you all know, is ambiguous, referring sometimes to a high official and sometimes to a low one. As I was ushered in to the office of the "secretary," I thought it might be some receptionist type, so I did not bother to ask the other men to accompany me. As I began talking to the gentleman, however, it gradually became clear that he was "the secretary," and I should have had the others with me. He forgave me, however, and that hurdle was presently passed.

"What you will need to do," he explained, "is to contact the Catholic and Protestant missionaries. They know a great deal about the tribal languages. Go to see them and get their opinion."

We already knew many of them. Some had been our students. How good it was, however, to be sent to them by the government! And when some of the Protestants criticized us for talking to the Catholics, we reminded them that the government had instructed us to do so.

Because the local university would be our sponsor if all went well, I felt we should ask them to assign one of their men to accompany us on our first trip to the interior. This the university was happy to do, but I kept wondering what misunderstandings might arise. Would the friendly young Indonesian anthropologist, even though he was a Protestant, comprehend and properly verbalize our presence in the communities we hoped to visit? Might he not compound potential problems by introducing misconceptions of his own? His English was none too good, and our Bahasa Indonesia was nil.

But the decision was made, and the university man became our guide. Wamena, the best-known town in the Irian Jaya highlands, was selected for our first stop.

I knew that it was important to report to local officials as the first order of business everywhere we went. As soon as the Twin Aztec landed in Wamena, therefore, I asked to be directed to the Chief of Police. We were told where to go. The university guide and I went and received a very friendly welcome. In fact, we must have spent nearly an hour enjoying refreshments which were served and telling about our plans. In the fractured combination of broken English and unintelligible (to me) Bahasa Indonesia, however, I missed a casual but crucial bit of information. After leaving the chief's house we were to go through the routine formalities of having our names, numbers, nationalities and destinations recorded in the office.

The remainder of the day was spent in a relaxed way, enjoying immensely the hospitality of the MAF couple who were our hosts. Because it had been a long and busy day, we all went to bed early.

About eleven p.m. a thundering of shouts, threats and hammering on the door was heard. I could not understand a word of it, nor did we have any idea what it meant. But our university guide did. "Where are the foreigners?" an angry policeman was demanding. "Why did they not register? They are illegal aliens and have broken the law!"

Now it was our guide's turn to talk. Not raising his voice as high as the policeman had done, he explained that the governor had sent us there, and that the university was sponsoring us, that we had credentials from Jakarta, and that we had spent an hour with the Chief of

Police that afternoon. It was not easy to mollify the policeman. The persuasion took a long time. But peace was finally restored. And how glad I was for our university guide and interpreter!

I am thankful to say that, though I have often fallen on my face, there *are* times when I let God help me do things right. The first trip Kay and I made into the Bru village where John and Carolyn Miller lived was such an occasion. The local pastor was expecting us and had refreshments waiting. And oh how we longed for them! But a sixth sense said, "See the District Chief first." We did. He was pleased. The pastor was greatly relieved that we had done so.

Debriefing

Every bit as important as checking in with the top official on arrival is checking out with him on departure. A friendly official in the Philippines told of having helped one of our men at the start of a survey trip. Then he added, "By the way, whatever happened to that guy? He never reported back when he returned."

When we wanted to work in Papua New Guinea, it was Alfred Coombe who started the ball rolling by getting an introduction for Bill Oates, Jim Dean and me to Paul Hasluck, who at that time was the Australian Minister for Territories. Mr. Hasluck introduced us to Brigadier General Cleland, who was the Australian Administrator for Papua New Guinea. But he was not in when we arrived in Port Moresby, so his assistant, Mr. R. W. Wilson, took care of us. "Dr. Groves is your man," said Mr. Wilson, referring to his Director of Education.

Dr. Groves did indeed prove to be God's man for the occasion. He assigned his Department of Education linguist to accompany us on a trip through the highlands which resulted not only in our choice of an area for the start of the work, but also in the choice of a site for our PNG linguistic center.

The last leg of our return flight to Port Moresby had to be started so early in the morning that we left without breakfast, and none was given us on the plane. When we finally reached the P.M. airport, therefore, we were famished. To my delight, cold pineapple juice and snacks had been provided by the airline for just such cases as ours. I dove for the refreshment table and returned to Bill and Jim with my hands loaded. To my annoyance, I found them talking to a man I did not recognize because the brim of his hat was down over his face. I was about to back off from the trio when the stranger turned to me. "How was your trip?" he enquired.

"Good," I replied, groping for some way to disengage myself in order to eat and drink. But the stranger continued to talk.

Suddenly I recognized him. It was Mr. Wilson! We were reporting back to our host, the Acting Administrator, who had started us on the journey. By the narrowest of margins God had kept me from a discourtesy which might have queered the good will we desperately needed to have from him. Before long our request for permission to work in Papua New Guinea was approved.

RSP

The Penny-wise and Pound-foolish

It was an emergency. A shocking earthquake had wiped out whole villages. The government had insufficient equipment to cope with the relief effort required. Could SIL help? Gladly!

JAARS equipment and crew reported to government. Work was given them and was properly done. Miraculously the flying even included enough non-emergency mileage to finance most of the emergency work.

Finally the disaster need was met and all could return to routines. But who would pay the four or five hundred dollar cost of the JAARS relief operation? "It is a golden opportunity," pointed out one of the JAARS men. "Let us pick up the tab." But someone sent a bill to the government instead. As suspected, it was not well received. At a time when all should have been sacrificing to meet a catastrophe for which no one nation was responsible, someone gave it a "business as usual" treatment. Thousands of pounds of potential good will were traded off for "pennies."

I had watched Uncle Cam buy cold Coca-cola for sweltering post office employees in Mexico as a means of helping generate good will and protecting our life-line in that important place, so I thought I knew what should be done when one of our members was having post office problems in a tropical town in another land. "If nothing else, give Christmas presents to the employees in that office," I urged.

"Sorry," came the reply. "I don't believe in it."

Result? Scores of Christmas greeting cards sent by that member, with expensive airmail postage to carry them to the home land, never reached their destination. The postage loss was far more than the Coca-cola or Christmas souvenirs would have cost.

The Reader's Digest tells how one experienced traveller keeps his cool over the various losses experienced by all travellers sooner or later. He includes in his budget a figure of 10 or 15 percent "for what I am going to be cheated out of." Then instead of blowing up when he is over-charged or loses money at some stage of his trip, he charges it up to that part of the budget. It is a canny contribution to peace of mind.

"He may work for money but must not accept pay for good turns," wrote a sage long ago. He was verbalizing a cultural universal. But some of us in each generation keep having to relearn it.

Jesus addressed the other kind of penny-wise with the words, "Why do you not rather suffer yourselves to be defrauded?"

RSP

The High Cost
of Short Circuits

When I was in charge of visas and importation paper work for one branch, a member fouled his visa up in such a way that under normal procedure it would have taken at least a month and a half to remedy it. On top of that, he wanted to leave the country the next day. My advice was simple, and had he followed it, things would have been all right. He did not want to go that route, so took the matter to the director and to my immediate boss. They sided with the member and asked me to short-circuit the ordinary route.

Since the private secretary of the man in charge of the Immigration Office was a good friend of mine, I went to him for help. He immediately assigned his own secretary to help me straighten out the problem. This man took me to five heads of departments and in a matter of two hours everything was taken care of. But at what a cost!

For two months I was no longer accepted as a friend by the fine men who were by-passed by the short cut. In fact, I completely lost the friendship of one of them. I had overstepped their authority in an area where outside pressure, especially from their top man's office, was not welcome. I had humiliated them, making them drop everything they were doing and pull some of their secretaries out to take care of "my" request. They had to stop their clock and give me their undivided attention. It hurt them especially when they saw their "friend" stand-

ing with the man who was "ordering" them to straighten
out the visa.

Jose Estrella

Alphabetical Index
of Articles with Descriptions

Topical Index